COLD MOUNTAIN BOMBER CRASH:

THE ENDURING LEGACY

Warm Mountain wishes,

Doris Rollins Cannon

DORIS ROLLINS CANNON

Inquiries should be sent to:
Katydid Chorus Books
Attn: Doris R. Cannon
P.O. Box 193
Smithfield, NC 27577

Printed by Edwards Brothers, Inc.,
Lillington, NC and Ann Arbor, MI

Cover design by Doris Rollins Cannon and Eric Huffman

Cover Photo by Reba Frady McCracken

Cover photos of servicemen courtesy of their family members
and Burton Historical Collection, Detroit Public Library

ISBN 0-9772101-0-3

CONTENTS

Foreword vii

Part One:
BOMBER DOWN!

The Mountain 1

Final Flight 3

Local Citizens Join In 10

The Recovery Process 13

A Terrible Task 16

Lost Men 17

Prayerful People 20

Service on the Mount 22

A Wheel Flies Once More 24

An Odd Cycle of Deaths 27

Part Two:
THE MEN WHO DIED
AND LOVED ONES
LEFT BEHIND

Major General Paul B. Wurtsmith 31

Lieutenant Colonel Fred L. Trickey, Jr. 46

Lieutenant Colonel Paul R. Okerbloom 73

Master Sergeant Hosey W. Merritt 90

Staff Sergeant Hoyt W. Crump 111

Part Three:
BACK TO COLD MOUNTAIN
AND THE REST OF THE STORY

No Rest for the Major 147

Lost Girls 151

Mack's Mountains to Climb 154

The Roy Moody Story 159

Acknowledgements 211

2011 Update 215

*To every thing there is a season,
and a time to every purpose
under the heaven;-*

Ecclesiastes--3:1

 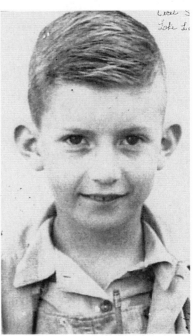

Doris Rollins, age 11   *Roy C. Moody, age 9*

1946

FOREWORD

On Friday the 13th of September, 1946, Cold Mountain in Haywood County, North Carolina became the scene of a terrible tragedy.

Five World War II heroes, who had begun to rebuild their lives following their harsh four years in the war, died instantly in a B-25 bomber crash near The Mountain's summit.

The dead were mourned and eulogized across the nation and in other parts of the world, and the scope of the disaster immediately drew hundreds of people of all ages to view the wreckage on The Mountain.

At the time of the bomber crash, I lived with my parents, Coran "C.S." and Lela Mann Rollins, my brother, Steve, and my grandmother, Mary Murray Mann, on Love Joy Road in beautiful Pigeon River Valley near Cold Mountain.

I knew that several of my sixth grade classmates had gone to the crash site, and I asked permission to go also, knowing full well what the answer would be. And after receiving the "Absolutely not," I pouted for my usual period of time and then became distracted by activities at school.

Among other children who were not allowed to go to Cold Mountain following the bomber crash was Roy Chambers Moody, age nine. He and his parents, Ned and Nell Chambers Moody, lived on Lake Logan Road, less than five miles from my home, and about the same distance from Cold Mountain.

Roy and I didn't know each other, because he was a fourth grade student at Cecil Elementary School in 1946, and later attended Hazelwood Elementary School and Waynesville Township High School in the same county, and I attended Bethel School near my home from grade one through 12.

Little Roy was crazy about anything with wheels, and by 1946 he already knew a lot about World War II aircraft. He begged to see the one that crashed on Cold Monntain, but his father said a firm "No," and that was that.

Roy's disappointment was severe, but he soon focused on other things with wheels, and the B-25 crash left his mind completely for an astonishing period of 32 years.

In the summer of 1978, his memory returned in full force as he looked through 1946 newspapers on microfilm in the Haywood County Public Library.

He began collecting all the printed material he could find about the crash and talking to people who went to the site in 1946. And through those and related activities, he became known as *Haywood County's Bomber Crash Historian*.

In early winter of 2004, I began looking through a tattered scrapbook of newspaper clippings which had been compiled by my grandmother, who died in 1959.

Grandmother didn't have a "store-bought" scrapbook or glue, so she made a paste of flour and water and secured the news articles in one of my father's agriculture textbooks from his days at State College in Raleigh.

I had thought of the bomber crash now and then through the years, but when I turned a page in the old scrapbook and saw the yellowed and crumbling report of what happened on Cold Mountain, the tragedy took on a new and urgent significance in my mind.

The front page story from a Haywood County newspaper listed only names and ranks of the men who died on The Mountain, and the fact one was a Major General in command of the Eighth Air Force. The General's first name was Paul, but the other men's first and middle names were listed only with initials. What was behind those names which had been read by my family, neighbors, and friends so long ago? Where did the five men spend their childhoods? What were they like in looks and personality? What did they do in World War II? Did they have wives and children, and if so what happened to them after the tragedy on The Mountain?

I decided to try to find answers to those questions. And since my grandmother had only written *1946* on the old news clipping, I needed to begin by finding the precise date of the crash.

So I made a phone call to John H. "Johnny" Rhodarmer Jr. in Canton in Haywood County. He had served in the Air Force and also the Marine Corps shortly after World War II, and had retired from a career with the U.S. Postal Service.

Johnny and several of his friends met for breakfast each weekday morning at McDonald's restaurant in Canton, and the group jokingly referred to themselves as *The Liars Club.*

When I asked about the date of the bomber crash 58 years earlier, Johnny said it was ironic that I wanted to know, because the crash date had been a main breakfast topic only the day before.

In addition to Johnny, those taking part in the discussion that morning were Air Force veteran C. Max Burnette; Army veteran Bob Paxton; and Marine Corps veteran Sam Henson, all retired from the Champion paper plant in Waynesville; Army veteran Jack Harkins, a long-time dairy farmer; and Robert Cathey, former chairman of the Haywood County Board of Education who had retired from a career with the U.S. Forest Service.

Johnny said a friendly argument about the bomber crash date had developed, and Max Burnette called his former co-worker, Roy Moody, who settled the dispute.

Therefore, Johnny put me in touch with Roy, and the roots of this book took hold.

By 2004, I had been a long-time resident of Johnston County, North Carolina, 300 miles from the home of Roy and his wife, Gail, in Waynesville.

And we were still strangers.

But after a few phone conversations about the bomber crash, we felt as though we had known each other since our childhood days near Cold Mountain.

Roy shared his newspaper reports, other printed materials pertaining to the crash, subsequent happenings on The Mountain in 1946 and later years--and how the crash effected a number of lives in Haywood County.

And for the first time, he revealed the amazing and inspiring story of how the long-ago disaster impacted his adult life.

Through regular mail, line phone, cell phone, e-mail, and the Internet, I spent over a year researching the lives of the men who died on Cold Mountain and their loved ones left behind. (As my task began, I remembered that homes in my native community had no electricity until the late 1930s and no telephones until the early 1950s, and I wondered what my grandmother would have thought about the tools of modern technology which were picking up where a faded page in her scrapbook left off.)

As my writing progressed, Roy continued to supply new information from his end of the line, suggested people and places to contact, and provided encouragement when some of my research trails led only to brick walls.

I shared each of my new findings with Roy and Gail, and the three of us were deeply moved, often surprised, and always inspired by the lives of Major General Paul B. Wurtsmith, Lieutenant Colonel Fred L. Trickey Jr., Lieutenant Colonel Paul R. Okerbloom, Master Sergeant Hosey W. Merritt, and Staff Sergeant Hoyt W. Crump--and their parents, siblings, widows, and children.

As the project came to a conclusion, Roy and I agreed that our efforts to record the history of the bomber crash and its enduring legacy had been blessed far beyond our initial hopes.

When this book went to press, the two "children" who were not allowed to go to the B-25 crash site in 1946 had still not met face-to-face, but their *purpose* (and *reason),* had been fulfilled.

---Doris Rollins Cannon

*Dedicated in honor of the five heroes
who died on Cold Mountain in 1946,
their remarkable family members,
the good people of Haywood County, N.C.,
past and present; and all who have
served, are serving, and will be
serving in America's Armed Forces.*

Part One:

BOMBER DOWN!

THE MOUNTAIN

Cold Mountain, located in Haywood County in western North Carolina, earned international fame as the title and centerpiece of Charles Frazier's 1997 best-selling work of fiction, and through the 2003 movie based on the novel.

However, The Mountain had already achieved a certain brand of fame among Native Americans who lived in the area many hundreds of years in the past, and also among the hardy white pioneers who settled there in the late 18th and early 19th centuries.

Cold Mountain's home-grown fame continued with later generations of avid hunters and hikers, and those who simply sat on their front porches and admired The Mountain up close or from afar.

Following the American Revolution, parts of North Carolina came under private ownership through state grants.

One of the first to be granted a major portion of Cold Mountain was Waightstill Avery, a resident of Morganton in Burke County, N.C. A brilliant and colorful man, he became North Carolina's first Attorney General in 1777 and is the man for whom the state's Avery County was named.

Waightstill Avery never lived near Cold Mountain, but several generations of his descendants, members of the Lenoir and Michal families, have been residents of the area since well before the Civil War.

Since the land grants of early post-Revolution times, other private citizens have owned parts of The Mountain, but by 2005 it was largely the property of the Federal Government and is part of the Pisgah National Forest and Shining Rock Wilderness.

It is part of the Blue Ridge Mountains and is southeast of the Great Smoky Mountains National Park, which covers thousands of acres of wilderness on the western North Carolina and eastern Tennessee border.

As it was in distant "Indian Territory" times, Cold Mountain has always been regarded as a generous friend, offering an abundance of wild game and berries in season, and incomparable beauty and spiritual uplift all through the year.

September in the western part of the Tar Heel State is almost always accompanied by skies of deepest blue, and each tree seems to become a stage for the annual loud, quavering, lonesome-sounding concerts by insects known as katydids. It is then that every true mountaineer experiences "the feeling of fall," a sensation that cannot be explained in words, and is more than mere knowledge of the calendar and a change in temperatures.

The feeling of fall is something primitive, harking back through countless centuries and whispering through blood and bones of summer's impending surrender to autumn.

For local residents and tourists who flock to the western North Carolina mountains in autumn, Cold Mountain and others stage a breath-taking show of colors--varying shades of red, yellow, orange, and brown, and in some years have even added astonishing lavenders and pinks.

Like its neighboring mountains, Cold Mountain is also stunning when wrapped in the snows of winter, the tender pale green of springtime, and the lush blue-screened emerald of summer.

When one stands before The Mountain, it doesn't look as high as its reputation. Its north side is draped with a prominent and graceful Swag which seems to draw one's attention from the fact that the official 6,030 feet of its summit makes it the third highest mountain in the region.

Those who know The Mountain's blessings best also know its dangers. Many are those who have become lost on it for short periods of time, or even for several days.

There are those who know that terrible weather can descend on Cold Mountain's summit without warning, while sometimes leaving its lower regions untouched. They also know that certain spots in the area seem to be uniquely subject to cloudbursts, sudden dangerous and terrifying rains that can cause flash-flooding and leave folks stranded unexpectedly, or even cause drowning.

In the waning days of 1946 summer, it was a Cold Mountain clad in dense fog, rain, wind, and occasional lightning that awaited visitors who had never had the good fortune to know the sweet September side of its nature, to walk amid its unspoiled wonders leading higher and higher.

It was a cold mountain indeed that awaited five World War II heroes whose only wish was to pass over The Mountain, others, and be at home base in Tampa, Florida by early afternoon.

*****

FINAL FLIGHT

Early on the morning of Thursday, September 12, 1946, a proud bird stood at MacDill Air Field in Tampa, ready to receive pilots, crew, and passengers.

It was a B-25 bomber, also called a *Mitchell,* having been named in honor of Billy Mitchell, the legendary World War I Army pilot who became known as "the father of the Air Force."

The B-25, a medium-sized bomber, was the most famous aircraft of World War II, having been used in the first bombing of Tokyo, Japan on April 18, 1942. That was the first strike against the enemy homeland after the Japanese attack on the American base at Pearl Harbor on December 7, 1941.

At a time when American morale was very low, a top secret mission was planned, and 16 B-25s took off over choppy seas from the deck of the U.S.S. Hornet, with a scant 400 feet from start to lift-off. The bombers were hundreds of miles from their targets in Tokyo, and there was no chance of returning to the ship.

In this extremely dangerous venture, which could be deemed a "suicide mission," the first bomber to leave the Hornet deck was piloted by the mission leader, Lieutenant Colonel James H. Doolittle, whose name became legend.

None of the 16 B-25s were lost over Japan. One landed in Russia and 15 landed in or were ditched in waters near Free China. Seventy-one of the 80 pilots and crewmen involved in the mission survived.

"Doolittle's Raiders" and their B-25 bombers delivered an unexpected and potent blow to the enemy--and greatly boosted spirits back home.

The heroic mission was the subject of a film hailed by critics as the finest war movie made during the WW II period. Released in 1944, *Thirty Seconds Over Tokyo*, starring Spencer Tracy, Van Johnson, and Robert Walker, was based on the memoirs of Captain Ted Lawson, one of Doolittle's B-25 pilots.

After the April day in 1942, the B-25 saw duty in every World War II combat zone flown by Americans, Dutch, British, Chinese, Russians, and Australians. It was originally intended for level bombing from medium altitudes, but was used extensively in the Pacific area for bombing Japanese airfields from treetop level and for strafing and skip-bombing ships.

The bomber weighed 28,460 pounds loaded. It carried 975 gallons of fuel and 30 gallons of oil at takeoff.

It had a span of 67 feet and 7 inches; a length of 52 feet and 11 inches; and height of 15 feet and 9 inches. Its clear nose was made of quarter-inch plexiglas.

The bomber's two engines produced 1,700 horsepower each. Maximum speed was 275 miles per hour with a cruising speed of 230.

Going from ground to cockpit required a climb of 12 feet.

More than 9,800 B-25's were built during World War II.

At an undisclosed location in 1942, a lone soldier stood guard beside a B-25 bomber as sunrise brightened the eastern sky. (Photo obtained through www.RareAviation.com)

World War II battles ceased in August of 1945, soon after President Harry S. Truman ordered a new and horrific weapon, the atomic bomb, to be dropped on the Japanese cities of Hiroshima and Nagasaki.

Hitler's German troops had surrendered in May of 1945, and the shocking power of the atom bomb brought the stubborn Japanese leaders to their knees. Americans rejoiced that the nation could live in peace once more, and those who had survived the War would soon be welcomed home.

However, the official "World War II period" extended through the end of 1946--and therefore the men about to board the plane at MacDill Field--the men who had achieved great things during the four main years of the War--were still very much part of it.

The B-25 that would soon head down the runway at MacDill Air Field was a silvery color, indicating it was an Army Air Force bomber, not a regular Army aircraft.

It was probably built in 1944, and may have not seen much, if any, action overseas.

Written in black on its side was the identification number 227.

At around 8 a.m. on September 12, 1946, seven men boarded the bomber and prepared for takeoff.

*This 1944 photo shows a bomber like the one that took off from
MacDill Field in Tampa on the morning of September 12, 1946.
(Photo obtained through www.RareAviation.com)*

The pilot was Major General Paul B. Wurtsmith, who had
marked his 40th birthday in August, the same month in which
he had been named temporary commander of the Eighth Air
Force.

The man in the co-pilot seat was Lieutenant Colonel Fred
L. Trickey Jr., and crew members were Lieutenant Colonel
Paul R. Okerbloom, an air inspector who was also a pilot, but
would not be in that role on that day; Master Sergeant Hosey
W. Merritt, the radio operator; and Staff Sergeant Hoyt W.
Crump, the flight engineer. All were stationed at McDill Field.

Passengers were Lieutenant Paul R. Koons and Sergeant Randle E. Sutton.

The plane's main destination was Selfridge Field near Detroit, Michigan, where the General would conduct a routine inspection.

When a stop was made at Bolling Field at Washington, D.C., in order for the General to take care of some additional business, Lieutenant Koons and Sergeant Sutton got off and didn't board for the rest of the flight, for reasons unknown at the time of this publication.

It is likely that other stops were made on the way to Selfridge Field, although there is no record of such. It was not unusual for forms to not be filed at every landing point.

While at Selfridge Field, General Wurtsmith had a brief visit with family members in Detroit, whom he had not seen in a long time.

That visit ended around 11 o'clock that night.

The return trip began around 9:11 a.m. on Friday the 13th of September, and the plan was to fly directly back to Tampa.

Before leaving Selfridge Field, Colonel Trickey again filled out the proper form and signed it, and listed General Wurtsmith as pilot.

Records show that at 10:57 a.m., the pilot of 227 (Wurtsmith) radioed in to Tri-City Airport, serving Kingsport, Bristol, and Johnson City, Tennessee. Bad weather was settling in, and it was reported that the pilot requested a lower altitude because of it. The official report stated that the pilot was on an instrument flight plan at 6,000 feet and requested further clearance.

It was reported that the Tri-City radio operator advised 227 that 6,000 feet was below the safe minimum altitude for the area and asked if a higher altitude was desired. The pilot radioed back that he was now on CFR (Contact Flight), or visual control, and requested clearance to continue to Tampa.

Atlanta Air Traffic Control advised Tri-City Control that 227 was proceeding under CFR, not IFR (Instrument Flight), and that there would be no further instructions if the bomber continued under visual control.

*****

It was still storming off and on, and there was dense fog on Cold Mountain, when several people living in the area heard and/or saw the B-25 bomber roaring its way southward.

On Old Michal Road off Cruso Road, which is part of Highway 276 in the Cruso Community section of Haywood County, brothers Bill and Roy Norris were trying to repair a leak, and were working under an eave at the home of their parents, Mr. and Mrs. Tom Norris.

Tom Norris was at his barn when he saw the B-25 fly over his property, and was so startled that he ran to his house and exclaimed, "That plane was way too low!" And his sons agreed.

Seconds after the bomber passed over the Norris home, a tremendous boom like thunder was heard.

Roy Norris looked at his watch. It was 11:20 a.m.

Up on Sorrells Creek near Cold Mountain, Lenoir "Beanie" Moody was doing repairs at the home of Joseph Burke (just below Daniel Boone Boy Scout Camp above Lake Logan), when what he thought was a mighty clap of thunder shook the entire house and jarred a two-by-four piece of lumber he was preparing to nail. He had never heard or felt thunder like that before.

Like the Norris men, Beanie Moody later concluded that the "thunder" was the B-25 bomber meeting its terrible fate on The Mountain.

Dick Rogers, who was too young to go to school, was running around outside his house when the loud boom sent him scurrying inside.

Grapevines in the Pigeon River Valley were laden that time of year, and it was not unusual for young people to stand under the vines and eat so many that they became sick. For that reason, Joe Sales had to stay home from his seventh grade classes that day, and he too recalled hearing the bomber on its approach to Cold Mountain.

On Love Joy Road near the foot of Hen Top mountain, Cold Mountain's nearest mountain neighbor to the northwest, C.S. Rollins was in a woodshed behind his house when he heard the loud roar of a plane, and he stepped outside to take a look. But it had already disappeared in the low, thick clouds.

He recalled that the plane's noise stopped abruptly instead of trailing off gradually, like the usual sounds of aircraft in that area. It was later assumed that, from his vantage point, any sound from the bomber's impact had been blocked by Hen Top mountain. (No part of Cold Mountain was visible from his home.)

Up on "Chinquapin," over two miles from Cruso Road, 75-year-old Byrd Pless was busy with an annual chore. He was a school teacher who had returned to the classroom at Cruso Elementary School for a year, because the World War II had created a shortage of young educators. But on that day in September, Byrd was covering corn in a "trench silo" when he heard what sounded like a dynamite blast in the direction of Cold Mountain.

And like everyone else, he soon learned the sound meant horrible tragedy on The Mountain.

*****

According to the official military report, the B-25 bomber hit Cold Mountain between 11:20 and 11:30 on Friday morning, September 13. It crashed in a heavily wooded cove near the summit on The Mountain's north side.

The report stated that the watch worn by Master Sergeant Hosey W. Merritt had stopped at 11:30 a.m.

The bomber sheered the tops off trees for around 700 feet, and hit a rock cliff at around 230 miles per hour. Fuel was ignited on impact, and a large area around the crash site was burned. The mangled wreckage and severed bodies of the five men on board, some burned beyond recognition, were strewn over a wide area.

How close had the bomber come to clearing Cold Mountain? The official military report estimated 500 feet, but reports of news media and others who visited the crash site ranged from 100 to 250 feet.

Some observers concluded that if the plane had been 50 to 60 feet to the right, it might have gone down with less damage.

When no further radio contact could be established with bomber 227 after 11:30 a.m., it was reported missing, and approximately 50 planes of various makes and sizes began combing the mountainous area from Bristol, Tennessee to Greenville, South Carolina.

It was like looking for the proverbial "needle in a haystack." And the weather continued to be nasty.

*****

LOCAL CITIZENS JOIN IN

By 1946, most residents of the rural communities near Cold Mountain had electricity and radios.

Some parents didn't allow any radio-listening other than religious programs and news broadcasts. More lenient fathers and mothers let their youngsters listen to the dramatization of fairy tales on *Let's Pretend* on Saturday mornings, and really fortunate youths could hear exciting mystery programs such as *The Shadow* and *Mr. Keen:Tracer of Lost Persons.*

And many adults enjoyed programs like *Lum and Abner,* with all the amusing happenings at the Jot-Em-Down Store in Pine Ridge, Arkansas.

However, news of World War II had been the chief topic of conversation since 1941, and interest in fighter planes and bombers and everything that had been used by the Armed Forces to bring about victory remained at a high level for many years.

At the home of Frank and Ruth Sorrells on Love Joy Road, the radio was not a thing used for entertainment, but it did bring news of the search for the missing bomber. And the family knew that small planes in the area were part of the mission.

And at daylight on Saturday, September 14, Frank Sorrells Jr., called "Junior," who was a senior at Bethel High School; and his older brother, Wayne Sorrells, struck out in the rain for Cold Mountain.

They wore their regular clothes and shoes. "Nobody had hiking clothes and boots in 1946," Junior's wife, Maxine, said, "and most of us didn't have a raincoat either."

The day before, someone in the community had noticed a trail of smoke fighting its way through the fog and rain on Cold Mountain. Nothing was thought of it, since campfires were common. But now that a bomber was missing and search planes were in the area, the smoke took on added significance. It might be a clue.

Crossing Hen Top mountain near their home, the two brothers hiked as fast as possible and often had to fight their way through thick growth.

When they arrived at their intended destination, the young men were not prepared for what they saw through smoldering fires and a cold gray drizzle that enveloped the scene like a shroud.

The only balm for their stricken emotions was the certain knowledge that whoever was on that doomed aircraft had died instantly.

Thank God, they had not suffered.

"We'd never seen anything like it, and hoped to never see anything like it again,"Junior Sorrells recalled. "We were scared, and got out of there as fast as we could."

No homes near Cold Mountain had telephones at that time, so the brothers hurried down Cold Mountain and up and across Hen Top and went to the nearest country store with phone service and called officials about their terrible discovery.

*****

By 7:10 the next morning, Sunday, September 15, the wreckage was spotted from the air by pilots of an AT-11 search plane, Captain James M. Poole and Lieutenant O.S. Long of MacDill Field.

When the word came down, a recovery crew was organized at Donaldson Air Field in Greenville, S.C., the military facility closest to Cold Mountain.

The man in charge of the process was Major Theodore J. Hieatt, an intelligence officer who only three days earlier had received a tip and launched a search in the mountains around

Maggie Valley in Haywood County for remains of a UC-78 Cessna, the military version of a commercial C-78, which had gone missing in 1944, and was believed to have crashed somewhere in the mountainous areas of North Carolina or Tennessee.

The lost Cessna was carrying four men, including three Army officers and a scientist from the massive government facility at Oak Ridge, Tennessee, which was part of the top-secret *Manhattan Project*, leading to development of the atomic bomb.

An unusual number of military plane crashes had occurred in the western North Carolina and neighboring areas in the early to mid-1940s, and Major Hieatt had already investigated enough of them to last most men a lifetime.

Born in Louisville, Kentucky in May of 1899, he had reached a point in life when he might have preferred to encounter mountains on leave as a tourist. But at age 47, the Major was preparing to hike up nearly 6,000 feet of Cold Mountain to find Lord only knew what.

When he called for volunteers to go to The Mountain, Kenneth Lindsey, a young serviceman from the small town of Clyde in Haywood County quickly offered his services. (His private hope was that he might be able to spend a little time with his family while he was in home territory.)

But Major Hieatt said "No." Lindsey had been on guard duty all night, and he needed fresher men.

Lindsey argued that some of the soldiers being chosen for the mission had been on weekend leave, which meant they had probably been up all night and in fact were not nearly as fresh as he was, even after pulling guard duty.

But the Major wouldn't give in. And Lindsey had to remain at the base.

*****

THE RECOVERY PROCESS

When the search planes began circling the top of Cold Mountain on Sunday morning, September 15, it signaled residents below that the bomber had been spotted. And some began hiking up The Mountain immediately.

That morning, James Harrison Messer and his sons, Verlin, James Jr., and Ernest, were putting out salt blocks for their cattle on Lou and Welch Singleton's pastureland on Hen Top mountain. There were 12 children in the Messer family, including three sets of twins.

James Messer and his sons normally didn't work on the Sabbath, but the cows needed salt, and therefore "the ox was in the ditch."

It was a good day for such a task because the foul weather had passed and the sun splashed over the mountains and Pigeon River Valley once more.

The Messers had not learned that the bomber crash had been located, but they knew something important was happening when they saw the small planes circling.

So they headed toward Cold Mountain, and at the Swag they hooked up with the Sorrells brothers, who were going up again.

When they neared the crash site, a search plane swooped low enough for them to see the face of the pilot. He flew straight at them, and waggled the wings in what they perceived to be a warning to "Keep away!"

Then the pilot dropped two weights with long orange streamers in an attempt to pinpoint the exact spot of the wreckage, but both missed the target. Then he began dipping the wings toward the crash site, and the Messers took that to mean he wanted them to hurry to it.

Pilots in the area were also in touch by radio with the recovery party preparing to head up The Mountain.

To find the easiest and quickest way to the crash site, the recovery team from Donaldson Air Field had the help of Pisgah Forest Ranger W.M Huber and others.

Local resident Carroll Pressley was at Crawford Creek when the military personnel turned off Cruso Road. He was asked if he knew the best way up Cold Mountain, and he led Major Hieatt and his men to the crash site.

They followed the Crawford Creek Road for about three miles to Lenior Creek. And from there, they followed an old hunters' trail up the two-mile-side of Cold Mountain.

Sometime between 2 and 3 p.m. on Sunday, those waiting at the crash scene looked down The Mountain, and saw the soldiers coming.

Some remembered the number as being between 20 and 30, and others remembered around 12.

Verlin Messer, by 2005 retired and living in the Jonathan's Creek section near Waynesville, recalled that when the first member of the military party arrived on the scene, he asked if any of the men on the bomber had survived, and when he received the obvious answer, he said, "Damn! I was sure hoping somebody would be alive."

The Major and other servicemen began searching those at the site for weapons or important things they may have removed from the bodies or the aircraft.

Verlin Messer's little brother, Ernest, who was nine-years-old, had his handmade slingshot in his pocket that day. It was his most prized possession, and Major Hieatt took it from him.

Ernest was on the verge of tears, but the Major assured him he could have his slingshot back as soon as everybody was searched. And he was as good as his word.

Rubber body bags were brought to the site and remains were transported to Bracey Funeral Home in Greenville.

First Lieutenant Rosario P. Drago, a young doctor stationed at Donaldson Field, was the medical examiner on the scene.

*****

A brief, but much-needed moment of "comic relief" for bystanders came when one of the military team arrived with a handful of plump, ripe huckleberries he had picked on his way up The Mountain.

"Are these things poisonous?," he asked.

The local folks were surprised, and quietly amused, to learn that someone could think that Cold Mountain's huckleberries might possibly be something other than the most delicious and nourishing things The Creator had ever made for consumption by mankind.

And it was a story they told for a long time.

*****

Kin McNeil, a prominent member of the Bethel community, was one of those who arrived early at the crash site, and he described the scene to a reporter for The Asheville Citizen.

The article quoting McNeil was picked up by United Press wire service and published across America and other parts of the world.

This photo of the crash scene was made by John Anderson of Brevard and published far and wide. This copy came from The Canton Enterprise.

A TERRIBLE TASK

The military personnel removed some parts of the bomber and all personal articles they could find, and left the rest to be cleared by souvenir-seekers.

Those who found personal items and anything else that appeared important were urged to contact the proper officials and turn them in.

Some turned them in and some didn't. And some didn't because they had no telephones and didn't know how to contact the proper persons. Some found small things they wanted to send to the families of those killed in the crash, but they had no idea where those relatives might be. They knew nothing about the men on the bomber except names and ranks that were published in the local newspapers.

At the scene of the tragedy, none of the onlookers envied the task of the men from Donaldson Air Field.

It appeared that some of the recovery team might have become fortified with some local "moonshine whiskey" before their Cold Mountain ascent. But even the teetotalers at the site couldn't blame them for seeking a little anesthetic, however ineffective and a potential problem in itself.

Their job was one of the most difficult that anyone could imagine. And it required that they try to block out thoughts of the men who had died at that spot and of their devastated families who would soon be receiving their earthly remains.

Some of the local citizens joined the military personnel in helping recover body parts. One who assisted with the process on Monday was McKinley "Mack" Ledbetter, a student at Bethel High School. On that day, the crash site became an important part of his life, and would continue as such as years went by.

*****

LOST MEN

At the time of the bomber crash, days were getting shorter and the sun hid behind the western mountains a little further to the south each evening.

And because the recovery party did not begin its Cold Mountain task until mid-afternoon on Sunday, September 15, the work had to be called off soon, in order for everyone to get off The Mountain before dark. (Three days would be required to finish the process.)

On Howell Mill Road in Waynesville, Elizabeth "E.B." Moody James and her husband, Robert "Bob" James, operated a boarding house, and their tenants at the time of the crash were men who were working on a road project in the area.

It was Sunday afternoon before Mr. and Mrs. James learned through a radio broadcast that the bomber had been found on Cold Mountain.

And in spite of the late hour, Bob James and boarders Ozzie Herman, Steve Verasco, and Waverly Ivey headed for The Mountain.

Darkness caught them coming back down from the crash site, and they found themselves in a real dilemma. They stumbled through dense undergrowth and treacherous terrain all night long. And when they finally found their way to the foot of The Mountain and to Highway 276 after sunrise, they were nowhere near the spot where they had left their vehicle.

The men were exhausted, scratched, cut and bleeding, and their clothing was torn to shreds.

Having a similar experience on Sunday were two members of the recovery party and a photographer, who became lost trying to get off The Mountain in the dark. Forest Service personnel didn't locate them until Monday morning.

*****

Back at Donaldson Air Field in Greenville, Kenneth Lindsey of Clyde, who had been denied a trip to Cold Mountain as part of the recovery team, was allowed to participate in a different aspect of the historic disaster.

He was one of those chosen to carry General Wurtsmith's coffin between two lines of Honor Guards and onto a transport plane bound for Detroit, where the General had said goodbye to his family only a few days earlier.

Death certificates for the five men were signed by Major Hieatt, Lieutenant (Dr.) Drago, and the Rev. Oder Burnette of Cruso community, a Baptist minister and school teacher who had the official duty of signing certificates for all deaths occurring in his section of Haywood County.

*****

In the days following the bomber crash and initial recovery, Cold Mountain was crowned once again with skies of deepest blue. Katydids resumed their sad serenades at nightfall, and large numbers of people continued to make the trek to the crash site.

Three days after the crash, Mack Ledbetter and his teenage friend, Bernard Singleton, took their mothers, Allie Ledbetter and Verlie Singleton, up The Mountain. Since the hike to the crash site and back would take most of the day, the women packed a picnic lunch to eat on the way home.

But after visiting the site, their lunch remained untouched.

Audrey Sherrill Burnette, a resident of Daffodil Lane, off Lake Logan Road, was a young teacher at Cruso Elementary School when the crash occurred.

She and her father, L.M. Sherrill; her 13-year-old brother, Phil Sherrill; and her 16-year-old cousin, Betty Jean Blaylock, went to the scene eight days after the crash, and ate many a huckleberry on their way up The Mountain.

Clifford Kuykendall of Cruso was among the large number of other local residents at the scene that day, as were Jack Frady, Beanie Moody, Louie Reece, Jerry Reece, and Lindsey Rogers, local hunters who were also looking for bear tracks.

But no one at the site had a desire for huckleberries or any other food on the way back down The Mountain and for quite a while after that.

Appetites vanished because the crash scene was still encompassed by the awful scent of burned flesh.

Ice had formed on top of Cold Mountain by November of 1946, when J.M. Long, who lived near Cruso Road in the Bethel commuhity area, and his cousin, J.N. Hyatt, hiked to the crash site.

J.M. had just returned home from Germany, where he served with the Army's First Infantry Division, and J.N. was fresh out of the Navy.

They had not expected to find a scene in home territory that seemed to belong in a foreign battle zone, but there it was.

The young men started up The Mountain about 2:30 in the afternoon, and like others, they had to find their way down in the dark and didn't get home until well after 10 p.m.

*****

Military reports stated the basic cause of the crash was "contact flight below minimum safe altitude" in bad weather.

But personal theories would abound and linger through the years. A woman who saw the bomber on its approach to Cold Mountain said there was a fire coming out of one of the engines.

Those familiar with the B-25 note that such is common with that type of aircraft when it is "throttling up," and would not necessarily be a sign of engine trouble.

Holt Thornton, who lives in the colorful community of Lizard Lick in Wake County, N.C., was a turret gunner on B-24 bombers and C-47 cargo planes during World War II. Now and then, he was allowed to pilot a plane because of his earlier training.

By September of 1946, he was out of the Army Air Force, but was living near Donaldson Air Field.

He said all bomber pilots were aware that sudden up-drafts and down-drafts in mountainous areas can lift a plane higher and also force a plane down.

And he said that when word of the crash on Cold Mountain was received, the general opinion around Donaldson Field and the town of Greenville was that it had to have been a mighty down-draft during the storm that spelled doom for the B-25, considering the extent of wartime experience and expertise of the men on board.

Since World War II was still fresh on everyone's mind, some in the Cold Mountain area would always believe the bomber had been sabotaged by enemy agents in America.

Ned Moody of Lake Logan Road, said, "There was just something mysterious about that crash, and somebody may solve that mystery someday."

But weeks and months faded into years and decades, and flying too low was the only cause of the tragedy reported in the news media.

*****

PRAYERFUL PEOPLE

As would be expected, the most prominent question was why the crash had to happen at all. Why did the five young men have to die in that manner, after everything they had been through in the War?

In private homes and the many houses of worship in Haywood and surrounding counties (large brick churches in the towns and many small white clapboard churches in the countrysides), there were ardent prayers for those who died and their loved ones left behind.

No one in the crash region knew the five men or their family members, but they did know that fathers, mothers, brothers, sisters, wives, and children somewhere beyond Cold Mountain were suffering a tremendous loss.

From behind pulpits came a reminder that people of faith were not supposed to question events, but should view it as part of a Greater Plan. In words of the old hymn, *We'll understand it better by and by.*

On Sunday, September 15, after word spread that the bomber had been found, many local residents went straight from church services to Cold Mountain, without bothering to change out of their Sunday attire. It didn't matter that they might have to buy a new suit or dress after struggling through briars and brambles.

John H. Rhodarmer, left, and Larry Rhodarmer, who lived near Canton, were among the men who didn't bother to change out of their suits and ties and slick-soled dress shoes before making the hard climb up Cold Mountain. They are pictured beside one of the B-25 engines. (Photo courtesy of John H. Rhodarmer Jr.)

SERVICE ON THE MOUNT

In 1946, Rev. Thomas J. "Tom" Erwin, who lived at the intersection of Love Joy and Lake Logan roads, was a part-time Baptist minister. And during that period he was also a teacher and principal at Cecil Elementary School. (His lengthy full-time ministry began in the 1950s.)

He and his wife, Maggie, had a daughter and three sons, including Paul Erwin, who had graduated from Bethel High School in 1945 and had secured a job at the Dayco Plant in Waynesville, which produced rubber products.

Paul recalled that his father didn't go to Cold Mountain on the Sunday following the bomber crash, like so many others had done.

That Sunday night, Paul and his friend and neighbor, Roy Reece, rode together to work the "graveyard" shift at the Dayco Plant, and by dawn on Monday morning, both were looking forward to getting to their respective homes and sleeping like bears in winter, at least until time for the noon meal.

But Rev. Erwin had other plans for their day. When the young men arrived home around 7 a.m., the minister said, "Come on, boys. We're going up Cold Mountain."

So the weary Dayco employees put off their slumber plans and headed up The Mountain with the man who carried the Bible.

When they arrived at the crash site, there was no one there but Forest Ranger Huber and two military men, who had guarded the place overnight and were sitting on a log eating C-rations.

Some of the area was still burning.

Opening his Bible, Rev. Erwin read scripture. And he performed a memorial service as moving as any funeral in a house of worship. It ended with a beautiful prayer--there in that high and silent place where the bomber had made its final landing--the place where the souls of five heroes had lifted off on what was believed to be the greatest journey of all.

Rev. Erwin didn't know if the men who died there were Protestant or Catholic or Jewish or of some other faith. He didn't know if they had any religious affiliation at all.

He only knew that they had served their country, and other nations, in a time of greatest need. And he knew they had been willing to die for the cause of freedom.

He knew he had been called to Cold Mountain to perform a service in their honor--and it was with humility and gratitude that he answered that call.

Rev. Tom Erwin during his days as a part-time Baptist minister and a teacher at Cecil Elementary School near Cold Mountain.

Not long after Rev. Erwin's memorial service, residents from the section known as The East Fork (of the Pigeon River) began arriving. Among them were young brothers Roy and Ned Norris and O.C. and Frank Chambers, and their friend, J.V. Plemmons.

By then, it was known that it was permissable to remove certain things from the scene.

Roy Norris searched through the rubble and found a shaving kit and a briefcase with two stars on each.

When he lifted them from the debris, one of the servicemen guarding the scene put his hand on the pistol at his side and said, "Hold it right there!"

He told Roy he could keep the shaving kit, but the briefcase belonged to General Wurtsmith, and it had to be returned to the proper authorities.

After receiving the briefcase, the two servicemen threw down their C-rations. One commented that it was the item they had been waiting for, and to his partner he said, "Let's get the hell off this mountain!"

And they did.

*****

A WHEEL FLIES ONCE MORE

Ned Norris, Frank and O.C. Chambers, and J.V. Plemmons thought a good souvenir would be one of the B-25 engines, but they quickly learned it was far too heavy for them to handle in any way.

So instead of an engine, the young men chose to keep one of the bomber's large tires as a souvenir--and they sent it rolling down Cold Mountain. It crashed and careened through stands of trees and shrubs for a certain distance, then hit a large rock that propelled it high into the air one last time.

The tire had to be sent rolling three times before the boys got it to a fairly good stopping point.

The next day, Ned went to the home of his parents, Mr. and Mrs. Tom Norris, hitched his father's horse and sled, and transported the tire to a spot where they could haul it in a pickup truck.

The huge plane crash souvenir was placed flat on the ground near a creek on the Norris property, because by that time the boys were too tired to deal with it further. They were young, and there were cute girls and other exciting things to draw their attention. They went on with their lives, and the B-25 tire remained by the creek for several decades to come.

A few days after the East Fork boys took possession of a bomber tire, three young men from the Dutch Cove and Morning Star communities near the town of Canton claimed the other.

William J. "Bill" Rhodarmer, Robert "Monk" Fisher, and Stuart Smathers rolled the other tire down The Mountain. It would remain at the home of John "Buck" Plemmons in the Dutch Cove near Canton for around 50 years.

(However, the tale of the two bomber tires would not end where they were placed in 1946.)

*****

On many Sundays following the crash and recovery, as many bomber parts as possible were collected by the four sons of Rufus and Edna Hargrove, and the son of Van and Retta Wells, all of Love Joy Road.

Carroll, Frederick, Frank, and Troy Hargrove, and Zene Wells were all students at Bethel School. They ranged in age from nine to late teens, and they would go up Cold Mountain as fast as their young legs would carry them after services at Bethel Baptist Church and Sunday dinner at their homes.

Troy Hargrove, the youngest of the group, recalled that they would go over Hen Top mountain and follow a goat trail almost to the crash site. They carried tools to remove small pieces of hardware from the bomber, items that were still scarce after the main years of World War II. And they also garnered more accessible souvenirs.

After all that hiking and intense collecting, the boys made it back home in time to clean up and attend the Sunday night church services with their parents.

Thomas Lynn Wells, 11-year-old son of Tom and Beulah Wells of Love Joy Road, was fascinated with airplanes of all kinds. And he went with his cousin, Zene Wells, and Troy Hargrove to the crash site a number of times and came home with a treasured collection, including a parachute harnass.

Not long after the crash, several members of a Boy Scout Troop sponsored by the First United Methodist Church of Canton, and led by Floyd E. "Ish" Lowrance, went to the scene. Among the Scouts were Jack Lyerly, Carroll "Gene" Devlin, Charlie Wilson, Rayvon Mabry, and Bobby Gilreath. The outing was part of their training in use of a compass.

Their first attempt to find the crash site failed, but young "Toad" Birchfield, who was familiar with the area, led them to it several days later.

The Scouts tied a rope around one of the bomber's heavy propellers and slid it down The Mountain on dry leaves. "It's a wonder some of us didn't get hurt," Gene Devlin said.

They mounted the propeller upright in concrete, and it was housed in the Scout Room in the Methodist Church basement for decades.

Someone made rings from a piece of the bomber, and Kenneth Underwood of Waynesville, a member of the Waynesville High School Class of 1953, recalled that he bought a ring and wore it for a long time in his pre-teen years, then lost it.

Around 1948, Willis Ted Inman, father of Ted Darrell Inman of Lake Logan Road, put a hydraulic cylinder from the bomber in his small bulldozer, and Ted Darrell kept other crash souvenirs through the years.

In Paul Erwin's workshop at his home on Cruso Road, a part from the plane was still functioning in 2005.

Decades after the crash, long-distance hiker Emily Michal Terrell of Cruso Road found (and later lost) a piece of the plane's hull, about the size of a standard sheet of notebook paper, in the east prong of Lenoir Creek.

Countless other pieces of the ill-fated aircraft were collected and kept by people who continued to live near Cold Mountain through the years, and also by those who moved away or came to the crash site from far-away places.

The fuselage, parts of wings, and the two engines remained on The Mountain for many years after the disaster, like ghostly hosts welcoming the thousands of visitors who made the journey to the site.

*****

AN ODD CYCLE OF DEATHS

In 1946, Haywood County's population was around 36,000. It was a time when industry was booming and jobs were available for anyone who wanted to work. But at the same time, there was not much traffic on the county's streets and roads. It was almost unheard of for a teenager to own a car. Students either walked or rode buses to school, and many plant workers were provided bus transportation. Two-car garages were as rare as two-headed geese, and it was not unusual for some families to not own a motor vehicle of any kind.

But wrapped in the mists of time, and the coincidences and ironies surrounding the B-25 crash, was an eight-week period, beginning six days before the crash, in which there was an unusually high number of separate accidental road deaths in Haywood County--eight in all.

And in addition, there was a plane crash in Arizona that claimed the life of a Haywood County native.

Including the deaths of the five men on Cold Mountain on September 13, there were 13 accidental deaths in Haywood County in eight weeks.

The cycle began on September 7, 1946, when 24-year-old Marion Mann Ross, daughter of Mr. and Mrs. Ray Mann of Canton, was killed when her plane crashed in Globe, Arizona. She had been a WASP (Women Airforce Service Pilots) during WW II, and had been out of service for a year. She was flying cargo for Globe Airplane Company when the crash claimed her life. Marion's body was returned home to Canton and was buried in Plains United Methodist Church Cemetery.

On September 10, three days before the bomber crash, a 1946 Ford from South Carolina was forced off the road when a Whiteway Taxi from Waynesville crossed the center line on Highway 276 near Cruso.

The car, which was carrying a load of tax-paid liquor destined for sale in "dry" counties, overturned. There were three men inside. Killed was 22-year-old Harvey J. Pittman, who had served in the Armed Forces during WW II.

On September 12, the day before the bomber crash, William H. Warren died of injuries received while trying to board a logging truck on Balsam Road near Waynesville.

Less than a week after he and his friends went to the bomber crash site and had to find their way off Cold Mountain in the dark, 33-year-old Bob James was killed in a car wreck on Highway 209 near Lake Junaluska. It was September 21.

In its own way, the James accident was eerily similar in nature to the bomber crash. Bob lost control of his 1941 "Woodie" station wagon in a sharp curve. The vehicle struck a large rock, went airborne, and almost crashed in the Pigeon River.

Bob was thrown out in mid-air. There was not a mark on his body, but he sustained serious brain injury and died four days later, on September 25.

On September 29, Henry Terrell of Bethel community was killed in a motorcycle accident. A 28-year-old Navy veteran, he had a wife and three-month-old daughter.

Henry and his friend, Lewis Wright, were traveling in a car on Cruso Road when they stopped to help a boy who was having trouble with his motorcycle. After the two young men solved the problem, they took turns test-driving the machine. And Henry's second turn proved fatal.

Vinson W. Leatherwood was killed when a pickup truck in which he was traveling collided with a Trailway bus at the site of "Charlie's Place" restaurant in Waynesville on October 5.

Ernest Leslie Davis died of injuries received when his bicycle struck a parked truck in Waynesville on October 12.

A pedestrian, Mrs. Liner Frady, was killed when hit by a car in Waynesville on October 19.

And on October 26, Milan Clay Heatherly, 13-year-old son of Weldon "Red" and Lucille Heatherly of Cruso, was killed when his bicycle and a car collided near his home.

(In less than six weeks, eight persons had lost their lives on and close by Cold Mountain--five men in the bomber crash and two men and a boy at Cruso at the foot of The Mountain.)

The dreadful cycle was broken in early November of 1946, when Kenneth Walker of Waynesville wrecked his truck on Highway 209, but his injuries were not serious.

Adding to the irony of the odd cycle of deaths is the fact that three of the nine Haywood County people who died during that eight-week period were related to the persons responsible for this book. Marion Mann Ross was a distant relative of author Doris Rollins Cannon. Bob James was the uncle of Roy C. Moody, and Henry Terrell was Roy's first cousin.

In its ever-returning tenderness, autumn laid wreaths of red, yellow, and gold above the new graves only a few miles from Cold Mountain, and around the sorrowful scene near its crest.

And when chilling winds snatched leaves from the trees, those looking toward The Mountain could see the bomber's silvery fuselage glistening in the sun, like a wintry beacon leading toward an unknown tomorrow.

The dead were mourned as seasons followed seasons in Haywood County, North Carolina--and in the places where families of Major General Paul B. Wurtsmith, Lieutenant Colonel Fred L. Trickey Jr., Lieutenant Colonel Paul R. Okerbloom, Master Sergeant Hosey W. Merritt, and Staff Sergeant Hoyt W. Crump were left to pick up the shattered pieces of their lives--and move on in ways they could not have imagined at the dawning of September 13, 1946.

*****

Part Two:

THE MEN WHO DIED ON COLD MOUNTAIN, AND LOVED ONES LEFT BEHIND

MAJOR GENERAL
PAUL B. WURTSMITH

A BOY NAMED PAUL

Paul Bernard Wurtsmith was born in August, 1906, the year his parents moved to a large house at 1415 Campbell Avenue in Detroit, Michigan.

Paul's father, Fred B. Wurtsmith, a native of Germany, was an engineer on the Pere Marquette Railroad.

Ella Wurtsmith, Paul's mother, was a tiny bundle of energy whose life was devoted to home, family, church and civic activities. She also worked in a law office for 14 years.

Paul was the oldest of the Wurtsmiths' three sons. His brothers were Frank Wurtsmith, who became a television executive and lived in Royal Oak, Michigan; and Ferdinand Wurtsmith, who became a dentist with offices in the David Whitney Building in Detroit. Dr. Wurtsmith later lived in Grosse Pointe, Michigan.

All members of the Wurtsmith family belonged to Holy Redeemer Catholic Church in Detroit, where Paul was an altar boy. (By 2005, the church had around 2,500 members.)

Paul received his early education at the Holy Redeemer Grammar School, and graduated from Cass Technical High School in Detroit.

In his teen years, he earned money through work as a copy boy for *The Detroit News*. And in his spare time, he worked on a hotrod Model-T Ford, thereby expanding his mechanical expertise.

After high school, Paul enrolled at the University of Detroit. His plan was to earn a degree in aeronautical engineering, but in 1927 he left the University to join the Army.

*****

A RAPIDLY RISING STAR

After qualifying for flight training at Kelly Field at San Antonio, Texas in 1928, Wurtsmith graduated with the rank of Second Lieutenant.

In his early years as a flier, he participated in air races with the best pilots in America, including the famed Charles Lindburgh, the first man to fly solo across the Atlantic. And it was said that Wurtsmith came in ahead of Lindburgh in one race.

In an air show in Columbus, Ohio, the fuel line burst in Wurtsmith's small plane, and he was drenched with gasoline. A small fire was started on one of the wings, but instead of bailing out, the young pilot stayed at the controls and brought the craft safely down--away from the crowded area.

If a spark of fire had reached him while he was aloft, he would have been incinerated along with his plane. Many noted that his thought was not of himself, but of the safety of those on the ground.

While Wurtsmith was stationed at Selfridge Field in Michigan in 1930, he captured the coveted *Mitchell Air Race Trophy.* (Like the B-25 bomber, it was named for famed World War I pilot Billy Mitchell.)

As a Captain, Wurtsmith was sent to the Philippines, and after the Japanese bombed Pearl Harbor on December 7, 1941 and America entered World War II, he became an ace fighter pilot. His hot handling of the controls earned him the nickname "Squeeze," which stuck for the rest of his life.

He was promoted to Major in 1941, and within an astounding period of only nine months he had become a Lieutenant Colonel, then Colonel, and had soared on to the rank of Brigadier General—at the age of 36.

He was the youngest General in the Army Air Force—and on his way to becoming a legend in the Pacific.

At age 36, Brigadier General Paul B. Wurtsmith was the youngest General in the Army Air Force, and also one of the best fighter pilots. (Photos from The Detroit News)

"A MOUNTAIN OF A MAN"

General Wurtsmith was a handsome man, but small in stature, having inherited height and weight genes from his little mother.

But it was said that to those who served under his command, he was nothing less than "a mountain of a man."

Ben Holleman of Palm Beach, Florida, who spent around 10 of his retirement years in the Cruso area near Cold Mountain, served as an aircraft mechanic under Wurtsmith's command in the Pacific.

He recalled that the General was very well-liked. He was a leader who was extremely proud of his men--and always let them know it.

General Wurtsmith had shown his metal many times prior to World War II, but the enemy didn't know what it was in for when Squeeze really began squeezing.

Under the supreme command of General Douglas MacArthur, Wurtsmith commanded the 49th Fighter Group, which gained fame as the first to be stationed overseas after the United States entered the War.

"The Forty-Niners," whose base camp was named "Detroit" in honor of their commander's hometown, defended Darwin, Australia against a merciless Japanese bombardment early in the War.

In woefully outdated aircraft, the Forty-Niners gained glory by shooting down 38 enemy bombers and 40 fighter planes, with loss of only 17 American planes and 12 pilots.

And Squeeze Wurtsmith was right up there in the middle of the action, becoming the first General to earn a *Distinguished Service Medal* in combat.

Early in 1945, he assumed command of the 13th Air Force in the Philippines, which was known as "The Jungle Air Force." It had a good record but needed to develop some long-range fighter and bombardment tactics, and do it in a hurry.

In short order, Wurtsmith's unit was striking the enemy in distant lands such as Batavia, Java, and French Indo-China with night-flying bombers, and at the same time maintaining a tight aerial blockade of the South China Sea, cutting off Japan's vital flow of raw materials from lands she had conquered in the south.

After the War, Wurtsmith was a 39-year-old with two stars --the lofty rank of Major General.

As his last big assignment, he took over advance headquarters of the Far Eastern Air Force, including the Fifth Air Force in Japan and Korea, and the Seventh Air Force in the Ryukyus--along with the post of Commanding General of the 13th Fighter Group, which had settled in the Philippines.

In August of 1946, he was named temporary commander of the Eighth Air Force--and there was much talk of greater things ahead for the man called Squeeze.

While the General was away at War, his wife, the former Irene Gillespie, lived in San Antonio. (How the two met is not known, but it is likely that they were introduced while he was stationed at Kelly Field.)

The General and his lady, Irene, were all smiles when he arrived in Detroit on leave in 1943. (Detroit News photo)

The couple's marriage was solid, and they wanted to have children. But that was not to be.

Margaret Wilcox of Michigan, who had been related to the General by marriage, said, "Not having children was a great disappointment for him."

General Wurtsmith, left, and his cousin, Naval Lieutenant Commander P.F. York, enjoyed a reunion in Detroit in 1945. (Detroit News photo)

A LAST GOODBYE

On September 14, 1946, Ella Wurtsmith was reported to be near collapse after being informed of the findings on Cold Mountain.

Her son had visited her only the day before--a never-to-be-forgotten gift for her 77th birthday. By that time, the General's father had been dead for seven years.

A huge number of friends and relatives had planned to attend a party on Mrs. Wurtsmith's actual birthday, which was September 14, but the General had chosen to come two days early.

It had been about three years since he had seen his mother and brothers, and he wanted them to have some time all to themselves--a little family together again after the horrible War--a mother and her sons on a pleasant late summer evening, without a thought that it would be a time of last goodbyes.

The shocking news from North Carolina changed plans for Ella Wurtsmith's birthday celebration to one of mass mourning in Detroit.

Many hundreds came to the Wurtsmith home on Campbell Avenue to give their condolences and grieve the terrible loss along with Ella and other family members.

It was said that, until the final word was received, the General's mother had held out hope that her son's plane had crash-landed safely and that all on board would be found alive.

The General would have been proud of his little mother, who quickly sprang back from the initial shock of his death, the mother whose faith carried her through her darkest times.

Just as her son had been seen in the eyes of the men he led, Ella Wurtsmith appeared tall and strong to all who came in contact with her after the tragedy on Cold Mountain, and they recognized that they were in the presence of a great lady.

*****

AT REST IN ARLINGTON

On September 18, 1946, General Wurtsmith's earthly remains were buried in Arlington National Cemetery, Arlington, Virginia.

The Funeral Mass was conducted in the Roman Catholic Chapel at Arlington.

Not far from his final resting place, in an almost straight line roughly the length of a football field, is the grave of Air Force Master Sergeant Wallace Pressley, who devoted 23 years to service of his country and was a veteran of the Korean and Vietnam wars. In his youth, he was a student at Cecil Elementary School and Bethel High School, and he lived on Lake Logan Road near Cold Mountain.

He was one of the many teenagers who went to the crash scene and brought home pieces of the bomber to keep through the years. He died in Dover, Delaware at age 57.

Also interred at Arlington are the ashes of Air Force Major General Roger K. Rhodarmer, a World War II bomber pilot who retired in 1973 as Commander of the Ninth Air Force. A 1940 graduate of Canton High School, he grew up in Kim's Cove near Canton, around 12 miles from Cold Mountain. And as a young officer he visited the B-25 crash site. He died in Columbia, S.C. at age 79 in 2001.

*****

A REPORTER'S TRIBUTE

Soon after the death of General Paul B. Wurtsmith, John M. Carlisle, a War correspondent, wrote about his personal recollections of the man called Squeeze.

In part, his article published in *The Detroit News* is as follows:

Some men of war who lead are feared, some are respected, and a very small few like Squeeze Wurtsmith are loved by the men who served under them.

He was one of the brilliant Air Force commanders of the Pacific, yet he was not a brass hat. He was a regular Army man, but he was not regular Army-minded. From Selfridge Field to Atsugi Airstrip in Japan, the GI's know they have lost a good friend.

Fighter pilots of the 5th, 13th, and 8th Air Forces, until the recent tragedy on Cold Mountain, would have bet a month's pay any time that he would have been Commander of the entire Air Force by age 50.

General Wurtsmith died at age 40, and if he had had a chance to have written a farewell note, he might have said, "NOT NOW!," for he had an unfulfilled mission in life.

We talked about it when I saw him last, when we went fishing off Diamond Head, in the aquamarine waters of Oahu in the Hawaiian Islands.

We were relaxing between tests Abie and Baker in the atomic experiments at Bikini. Wurtsmith was an observer on the USS Blue Ridge at Bikini.

"All I want to do,' he said, "is live long enough to convince the American public that those days in Darwin, Australia must never happen again. We held our fighter planes together with bicycle tape, and everything the Japanese threw at us was better than what we had. We must never be caught in that fix again. Why, I remember when I hated to send up our boys of the 5th Fighter Command.

"I remember when we couldn't ask for supplies and parts--because there were none. I remember when pilots descended on a cracked-up plane like scavengers, all fighting for parts. I'm going to tell that story as long as anyone will listen."

In the Hollandia campaign, General Kenny, commander of the Far East Air Force, decided to use Filipino guerillas to get an airstrip ready before the attack was made.

General Wurtsmith volunteered, and General Kenney asked, "You know what you're doing?" He said he had in mind an officer of lesser rank and ability--a man who was more expendable.

Squeeze Wurtsmith answered, "I know. But if my boys are going in there, I know what they need--and I'll get it for them."

(What came next illustrated the General's sense of humor.)

When 'his boys' came in, Squeeze was waiting for them, and the first thing he said to a pilot was, "Joe, did you bring any coffee?"

While the War was still on, correspondent Carlisle went with Brigadier General Thomas "Tommy" White, commander of the Ninth Air Force, to Leyte, headquarters of the 13th Air Force, for a visit with General Wurtsmith.

By that time, the 13th had fought all the way back with General MacArthur.

Carlisle wrote: *Squeeze took off in a P-51 in a blinding tropical rainstorm, and General White watched him go. He grinned and said, "There goes the sweetest guy in the world--and what a guy!"*

When we got to Leyte, Squeeze was furnishing ground support for the 13th for the Aussies in the attack on Borneo. He was also running an air cargo line to Australia and back.

He said, "I have to have fresh vegetables and fresh eggs for my boys," and turning to General White he added, "Tommy, I always hated to fly on a stomach full of canned goods!"

Carlisle spent a month with the Jungle Air Force. He flew the Equator six times with General Wurtsmith, once on a 7,000 mile inspection trip of the 13th Air Bases.

On one flight in a "Fat Cat" B-17, a young flier from Detroit asked if he could go in the cockpit and "see the General for just a minute."

They ended up talking for four hours.

Later, General Wurtsmith told Carlisle, *"I got homesick, and that flier from Detroit was a swell kid."*

*****

WURTSMITH AIR FORCE BASE

In 1947, the Army Air Force emerged from under the Army's umbrella. And General Wurtsmith's heroic record was further enhanced, because he had played a large part in the United States Air Force coming into its own as a separate branch of the Armed Forces.

On July 4, 1953, almost seven years after his death on Cold Mountain, the General's entire legacy was honored in a special way.

An Air Force Base in his native state was named for him.

Wurtsmith Air Force Base at Oscoda, near Lake Huron on Michigan's Upper Peninsula, came into being in 1920 as the Army's Camp Skeel.

As a young Captain at Selfridge Field, Wurtsmith had led a group of small-plane pilots to Camp Skeel, to do research on how to keep aircraft in flying status in near-arctic tempertures. He and his fellow pilots spent three harsh winter months there, and as might be expected, their mission was a success.

In 1942, Camp Skeel was renamed Oscoda Air Field and became a P-47 fighter base.

The famed "Tuskegee Airmen," an all-black fighter squadron, trained for many weeks at Oscoda before going into action in WW II.

The field was closed for two years, 1945-1947, but was reopened due to heavy fighter traffic from Selfridge Field.

And the distinguished fighter base soon became home of one of the Strategic Air Command's most outstanding B-52 bomber wings.

Thousands were on hand for the Fourth of July renaming of Oscoda Air Field as Wurtsmith Air Force Base in 1953.

Among special guests for the dedication were General Wurtsmith's mother, Ella; his widow, Irene; and his young nephews, Paul D. Wurtsmith and Fred Wurtsmith.

Squeeze's old friend, General Tommy White, who had earlier called him "the sweetest guy in the world," was on hand to declare that the base was being named for the man who "was probably the best fighter pilot and fighter tactitian in all of World War II."

General George Kenney was also there to speak of the hero whose name would be carried by the base into an uncertain American future.

And the base lived up to its name in more ways than one.

In 1960, Wurtsmith Air Force Base became home of the 920th Air Refueling Squadron, with WKC-135 stratotankers.

As part of the Strategic Air Command (SAC)--it was set up to respond to nuclear attack by the Soviet Union.

In 1965, the KC-135 tankers from Wurtsmith AFB began flying "Young Tiger" missions in support of combat operations in Southeast Asia.

It was home to bombers with short-range missile capacity by 1974, and in 1980 the base was chosen for nuclear-armed Cruise missiles to equip its B-52 bombers.

Wurtsmith Air Force Base's 379th Bombardment Wing was named best in the Eighth Air Force in 1981, and in 1987 it was named the best B-52 and KC-135 Unit in the Strategic Air Command.

In fact, so many high honors were earned by those serving at Wurtsmith AFB through the years that is is not possible to list them all.

In 1990, staff personnel from Wurtsmith AFB were sent to Saudi Arabia to prepare for B-52 operations in Operation Desert Storm, which forced Saddam Hussein's Iraqi troops out of Kuwait.

But times were changing, and changes would soon filter down to the base named for the young hero General who died on Cold Mountain.

*****

MOTHER OF THE YEAR

The year after Wurtsmith Air Force Base received its name, General Wurtsmith's mother was named the 1954 *Michigan Mother of the Year.*

One of the letters recommending her for the honor came from General Douglas MacArthur.

By then, she had been a widow for 15 years, and had lost two of her three sons.

Dr. Ferdinand Wurtsmith died in 1949, only three years after his brother's death on Cold Mountain.

But little Ella Wurtsmith carried on, undefeated by life's harsh blows.

On September 14, 1959, *The Detroit Free Press* ran a story on the occasion of her 90th birthday. Written by James Hart, it reads, in part, as follows:

Mrs. Ella Wurtsmith rearranged the flowers throughout her 10-room house today--her 90th birthday. The actual celebration was yesterday afternoon, when nearly 200 friends and relatives came to the big house on Campbell Avenue to pay their respects.

Mrs. Wurtsmith, wearing a purple orchid on a blue dress, couldn't understand all the fuss.

"I don't think being 90 is so important," she said. The little lady--she is five feet tall and weighs 112 pounds--lives one day at a time.

"None of us know what will happen tomorrow," she said.

Mrs. Wurtsmith is a member of the Holy Redeemer Church, Catholic Study Club, University of Detroit Women's Guild, Providence Hospital Auxiliary, and League of Catholic Women.

She has lived in the same house since she and her husband came to Detroit in 1906.

The reporter concluded the interview by asking the late General's mother about her formula for living. And she replied that it was a simple one: *"THY WILL BE DONE."*

General Wurtsmith's mother received a kiss from her grandson, Fred Wurtsmith, during her 90th birthday celebration on September 13, 1959. (Detroit Free Press photo)

At age 91, Ella Wurtsmith died on May 1, 1961. Funeral Mass was held in Holy Redeemer Church in Detroit, and burial was in Saint Joseph Cemetery in Monroe, Michigan.

General Wurtsmith's widow, Irene, married Colonel James Duke several years after the bomber crash on Cold Mountain. The last years of her long life were spent in Sun City, Arizona. She died in 1990.

*****

LIEUTENANT COLONEL
FRED L. TRICKEY JR.

A BOY NAMED FRED

Fred Logan Trickey Jr. was born on June 30, 1915 in Berlin, Wisconsin. His parents were Army Major Fred Logan Trickey, who was born in 1867 in Washington, D.C.; and Grace Glenson Sells Trickey, who was born in Topeka, Kansas in 1878.

A marvelous midlife surprise, Fred Jr. came into the world when his father was 48-years-old and his mother was 37.

Grace and Fred Trickey's only other child was a daughter, Dorothy, who was 18-years-old when her little brother was born.

After college, Dorothy Trickey Swetting was a member of the teaching staff at Frances Shimer College at Mount Carroll, Illinois for several years, and later was a professor at LaVerne College in California.

Dorothy's only child, Margaret Swetting Heiss, was born when Fred Jr. was still a child.

*****

Early in life, Fred Jr. exhibited leadership abilities, and at Berlin High School he was an outstanding student.

He was a handsome young man with dark hair and dark eyes. He was not tall, but had a strong athletic physique.

During his four years of high school, he was elected class treasurer, vice president, and class president, and was on the Honor Roll each term. He was an actor in his senior class play, and a member of the band and orchestra, debating team, and Science and Latin clubs.

He played basketball and football for four years, and was captain of the football team in his senior year. He also played baseball for a year, and ran track for two.

As the BMOC (Big Man on Campus), Fred Trickey Jr. made girls' hearts flutter, and enjoyed that aspect of his young life.

Beneath his senior photo in Berlin High School's 1933 *Mascoutin* Yearbook is written: *"Twinkle, Twinkle, Athletic Star, You Love the Girls Where're You Are."*

After high school, he attended Ripon College, Chattanooga University, and Wisconsin University, but did not complete a degree. While at WU, he began preparing for service in the Army Air Force, and joined in July of 1940.

He became a pilot, and completed training with the 94th Pursuit Squadron at Selfridge Field in Michigan.

It was written that being a member of the 94th was in itself a high honor, because it carried the highest traditions of the Air Corps. It was the same unit that had been under command of Captain Eddie Rickenbacker.

(A native of Columbus, Ohio, Rickenbacker was a popular racecar driver who became a legendary fighter pilot in World War I.)

In the early days of World War II, Fred Trickey Jr. was assigned to the Ferry Command, later called the Air Transport Command. He flew and led flights to Russia, Africa, Australia, and outlying Pacific bases.

Duties of his unit were to deliver planes fresh off production lines to advance American and Allied bases.

While flying the southern route to Africa by way of Brazil, Trickey had the first of several emergencies which called forth his bravery and expertise.

On a small field in Brazil, one of his plane's engines faltered during takeoff, and with the added weight of extra fuel tanks, the craft was pulled toward the ground.

Only quick and decisive action on the young officer's part saved his life and lives of his crew in the resulting crash landing.

Not long after that, he began service in the 497th Bombardment Group of the 20th Air Force, and would continue to distinguish himself throughout World War II.

*****

A BITTERSWEET APRIL

In *The Waste Land*, poet T.S. Eliot defined April as *the cruelest month.*

It is then that the cold gray winter has passed, and the earth becomes green with life once more. The "cruelty" for mankind is that trees put out new leaves and flowers bloom in their annual splendor--but nature does not allow loved ones to return from their graves through the nurturing warmth of spring.

For the Trickey family, the spring of 1944 delivered a bittersweet kind of April with events that, in later years, would bring forth the feelings that the poet expressed so well.

In April of 1944, the bitter part came with the death of Major Trickey's father. And in the same month, and the sweet was added with the marriage of the Major and a Southern girl named Peggy Lorraine Clark.

Fred L. Trickey Sr. died at age 77 on April 25, and was buried in what was the first of five graves in the family plot in Oakwood Cemetery in Berlin, Wisconsin.

He did not live to know the outcome of World War II, or learn of all the heroic deeds of his son.

But he knew without doubt that his boy was capable of great things.

*****

On an unknown date in April of 1944, the wedding of Major Trickey and Peggy Clark took place in a Presbyterian Church in Memphis, Tennessee.

The bride, a 25-year-old auburn-haired beauty with hazel eyes, was born in Nashville, Tennessee on September 19, 1918. She was the daughter of Clifford and Nina Leech Clark

Peggy's father was a member of the Army Corps of Engineers, and therefore she was somewhat familiar with the rigors of military life.

She was aware that being an Army Air Force wife would present many challenges, especially in wartime--but she also knew she could meet them head-on.

Challenges were nothing new for Peggy Trickey. She had had a serious heart condition for years, but was determined to keep it from dictating the paths of her life.

Her strong spirit of independence and determination was demonstrated in many ways in her youth. One example was that she didn't like the first name she had been given at birth, and when she became of legal age, she had it changed from *Hazel* to Peggy.

She changed it to Mrs. Fred L. Trickey Jr. in a simple ceremony on an April day brimming with smiles, laughter, and hope.

*****

In the only wedding snapshot found in later years, the bride and groom are riding in an Army Jeep, driven by an unidentified friend of Major Trickey. The only other passenger is the maid of honor, also unidentified.

The bride is radiant in her white gown and veil, and the groom is wearing his white dress uniform and hat.

But in what some might view as an omen, Major Trickey's face is blocked out of the picture, and there are dark clouds on the horizon.

*****

There was joy on the April day in 1944, when Major Fred L. Trickey Jr. (face hidden) and his bride, Peggy, rode into matrimony in an Army Jeep.

*****

For the young Major in his bittersweet April of 1944, there was little time for mourning his father, comforting his widowed mother, or honeymooning with his bride.

There was a War to win, and he headed back to his duties as a B-29 bomber pilot and commander of the 870th Squadron of the 497th Bombardment Group, based on the island of Saipan in the South Pacific.

But the rigors of duty on Saipan seemed lightened when he received a letter from the States in early summer of 1944.

He was informed that he was going to be a father!

Major Trickey called his wife "Peg," and he was thrilled by the news that her lovely figure would soon develop a rather ponderous sign of something wonderful in their future.

He was so thrilled, in fact, that he renamed his bomber PONDEROUS PEG. And on the side of the plane he added a slight bulge to the tummy of a typical World War II pin-up representing his beautiful wife astride a bomb.

It was obvious that Peggy Trickey's sense of humor was fine match for her hero husband's.

*****

On a base on Saipan, Major Fred L. Trickey, left, and his crew posed by his B-29 bomber, PONDEROUS PEG, named in honor of his expectant wife.

54

*****

On December 22, 1944, Major Trickey flew an extraordinary bombing mission over Tokyo, and was later honored with the *Distinquished Flying Cross.*

The story of that mission was reported in the history of the 497th Group, as follows, in part:

The most amazing flying accomplishment during the month (December) was the feat of Major Fred L. Trickey, in coming home from a mission with two engines—both on the same side.

(The two on the other side had been shot out by ground -fire.)

After he lost the second engine, Major C.C. Fowler, pilot of a nearby plane, radioed Major Trickey and told him that he would accompany him back to Saipan.

Major Fowler suggested with two engines on only one side, his plane was in no condition to make it back to home base. And he advised Major Trickey to ditch it while it was still daylight.

At the time, the two planes were not far from Iwo Jima.

Major Trickey radioed back to Major Fowler and told him he was about to see a plane get back in condition to make it home, and to everybody's surprise and gratification Major Trickey accomplished his goal and piloted his crippled bomber safely to home base.

*****

In the winter of 1945, Major Trickey received the news that, with the exception of a heart heavy with joy, his wife Peg was no longer ponderous.

The couple's child, a boy, was born on February 26. Mother and son were doing fine, and the little one was named Fred Logan Trickey III.

*****

By August of 1945, the father of little Fred III had advanced to the rank of Lieutenant Colonel, and he received news that he was to be awarded a *Silver Star* for gallantry in action on May 23 of that year, when he still held the rank of Major.

At that time, he was commander of a B-29 flying from a base in the Mariana Islands on a night incendiary bomb strike against Tokyo. The goal was to set fires, and the official description of what happened is as follows:

At landfall, heavy anti-aircraft fire was encountered, continuing all the way to the target.

On the bomb run, a malfunction in the bomb release system prevented the bombs from being dropped. Despite the intense anti-aircraft fire, numerous fighter attacks, and many searchlights, Colonel Trickey, determined to bomb the target, brought his airplane in on a second bomb run.

Again, the release system failed to drop the bombs, and as the aircraft proceeded on, it was coned by 30 searchlights and subjected to an intense and accurate barrage of anti-aircraft fire and attacks by enemy night fighter planes.

Two engines on the same side were heavily damaged by flak and had to be feathered almost immediately.

The right landing gear was also damaged by flak and the landing gear doors fell open.

The number four engine caught fire and burned for several minutes before being extinguished.

The aircraft was losing altitude rapidly, but through his superior ability Colonel Trickey was able to level off the bomber at low altitude.

Shortly after land's end, adverse weather was encountered, and with several instruments shot out, two engines inoperative on the same side, and the drag of the open landing gear doors, the long return flight over water seemed impossible to accomplish successfully.

The heavy battle damage necessitated landing at an emergency field, but as the base was reached, the weather was so adverse that Colonel Trickey was forced to circle the island for nearly two hours before a landing could be made.

When a break in the fog was observed, Colonel Trickey brought his aircraft in, effecting an excellent landing without further damage to his plane or injury to any crew member, despite the fact that both right landing gear tires were flat as a result of anti-aircraft fire.

Colonel Trickey's professional skill, courage, and devotion to duty are in keeping with the highest traditions of the Army Air Force.

Colonel Trickey's citation was by order of Lieutenant General Nathan F. Twining, commander of the 15th Army Air Force.

Upon learning that he was going to be awarded the *Silver Star*, Colonel Trickey sent word to command headquarters that he would not accept such an honor--unless every member of his B-29 crew received the same.

And they did.

Colonel Trickey received another *Distinguished Flying Cross* in October of 1945.

(After various medals are awarded, additional ones are represented by Oak Leaf Clusters, Palms, or Stars.)

The Colonel's Oak Leaf Cluster for his second Distinguished Flying Cross was for action that took place on April 24, 1945.

He was Acting Wing Commander on a low-level, daylight raid against the Hitachi aircraft plant at Tachikawa, Japan, described as follows:

Despite intense and accurate flak and persistent, aggressive fighter attacks, Colonel Trickey led the Wing over the target so skillfully that the bombing results were severe damage to the plant. Strike photos show that over eighty percent of the target was destroyed.

Colonel Trickey's display of leadership, coolness, courage, and ability under fire was a distinct contribution to the success of the mission, and reflect great credit on himself and the Army Air Forces.

Before World War II ended, Colonel Trickey had flown 34 battle missions and three supply-drop missions over the Japanese homeland.

In addition to the Distinguished Flying Cross with one Oak Leaf Cluster and Silver Star with Palm, the Colonel was recipient of a Presidential Unit Citation with one Oak Leaf Cluster, the Air Medal with four Oak Leaf Clusters, and the Pacific Theatre Medal with four Battle Stars.

He returned to the States for good shortly before Christmas of 1945, around four months after the Japanese surrender, and proceeded with plans to separate from the Army Air Force and begin a life career in the regular Army.

Welcoming him home in Tampa were Peg and Fred III, who was almost 10-months-old.

The Colonel attended the Army Command and General Staff School at Leavenworth, Kansas, and graduated with the rank of First Lieutenant, while retaining his Reserve rank of Lieutenant Colonel.

He was happy to have the War behind him and to be able to really begin life with his wife and son.

*****

On an evening out with Peg, Colonel Trickey showed the photographer just how glad he was to be home.

Happy days in The Sunshine State followed for the little family, and their future seemed to stretch far beyond the palm trees and blue ocean horizon.

And in the spring of 1946, Peggy Trickey was beaming when she announced that she was going to "update" the name of her husband's wartime bomber.

She was going to become ponderous again. The couple's second child was on the way.

In this last known snapshot of Colonel Fred L. Trickey Jr., his wife Peggy, and son Fred III, the little family enjoyed an afternoon in the Florida sun in the summer of 1946.

THE WORLD TURNS UPSIDE DOWN

On September 13, 1946, Peggy Trickey, then in the fifth month of her second pregnancy, called her mother-in-law, Grace, in Wisconsin and told her that the B-25 carrying Colonel Trickey was reported missing.

And the next day, the Trickey family's world turned upside down.

Lieutenant Colonel Rod Francis, a close friend of Colonel Trickey, contacted his mother and broke the awful news that her son's remains had been found amid the bomber wreckage on Cold Mountain.

The highly-decorated war hero was dead at age 31.

In Tampa, the couple's many friends rushed to offer comfort and support. The irony was that Peggy did not know the other men on the plane or their grieving widows at the base, because members of the B-25 crew on that tragic September 13 were not members of Colonel Trickey's regular crew.

Shortly after news of the tragedy, Peggy and her small son went to Wisconsin to be with the Colonel's mother and prepare for his funeral.

At age 18 months, Fred L. Trickey III was fatherless, and too young to grasp the meaning of what was taking place.

*****

BACK TO HOME BASE, BERLIN

When Colonel Trickey's coffin arrived in his hometown, his mother was distraught upon learning that it could not be opened for viewing of the body.

Colonel Rod Francis had accompanied the casket and would remain with the family through the funeral. And as gently as he could, he explained to Grace Trickey that the nature of the bomber crash was such that there was not much more than a uniform in her son's coffin.

Colonel Trickey and Peggy would have celebrated her 28th birthday on September 19--but instead she attended his funeral on that day.

The Trickeys were Congregationalists, and the funeral was held in Union Church in Berlin. A huge crowd came to bid goodbye to the young man who had been, and would continue to be, the pride of Berlin and the entire state of Wisconsin.

Pallbearers were the Colonel's close friends in the 497th Bombardment Group. They were: Major J.B. Lampley, Major P.L. Yon, Major J.C. Arnold, Major H.G. Walker, Major J.T.O. Archer, and Captain Keith Whitaker.

Colonel Trickey's Flag-draped coffin was surrounded by flowers and backed by a huge gold and purple arrangement in the form of wings--the Army Air Force emblem.

The service was conducted by Rev. Arthur W. Sneedsby, who had been the Trickey family's pastor for many years.

As the Colonel's young widow placed a protective hand over their unborn child, and held their small son close, she listened to the minister's words as follows:

We do again pay a high and precious price for our progress in mechanical science, and our leadership in airborne travel.

To the bereaved hearts, the loss of a son, a husband, a father is well nigh intolerable. To the public at large, it is the wear and tear of the wheels of progress.

There is no adequate explanation in Providence for such tragedies, but they reveal the fact that our science and human endurance are far from perfect; that our human existence is subject to the forces of gravity and momentum as well as to disease and violence.

Gradually and slowly, we are mastering our enemies, but at present there is enough of their mastery over us to send us to the sheltering arms of Eternal Grace. And He who created the genius of man and gave him the dauntless heart by which he makes and flies his planes, will also grant us grace and courage to face and bear the cost of genius and dauntlessness.

Divine Providence does not keep his loved ones from these tragic experiences; but He does keep the soul in them.

Man was not made to be safe. He was made for creativeness, conquest, for climbing, for growth and progress. In this, he shares the nature of Him who made him.

Another brave, intrepid spirit has made his mark across the landscape of our lives. We mourn the loss of Lieutenant Colonel Fred L. Trickey Jr., too fine to be lost, too young to die; but we thank God for his great and gallant services; his great and friendly heart; for the boy he was, for the man he was; and now for the memory of his laughter, his life and love; for his skill, his patriotism, and his dauntless spirit.

In closing, Rev. Sneedsby read the following poem:

*There is no sanctuary for brave
    men,
Danger allures them as if it were the
    sun.
What they have dared, they will
    dare again;
And shall continue until the day
    is done.*

*There is no satiation of brave
    deeds,
One draws another as wit calls on
    wit.
Oh what a soul it is that ever
    heeds
The hour's necessity and springs
    to it.
There is no sanctuary for brave
    men.
Danger allures them as the moon
    and the tide.*

*What they have dared, they will
dare again--
Though they lose all else in the
world beside.*

At the Trickey family plot in Berlin's Oakwood Cemetery, a squad of Veterans of Foreign Wars fired three volleys of a 21-gun salute over Colonel Trickey's grave.

Taps, also known as *The Soldier's Farewell*, was played by Helen Richter, and as the bugle's final note faded, a distant echo came from a bugle played by Victor Wiecki.

Mourners left the grave of the hero who died too soon with the final notes lingering in their minds, along with the words of the first verse, which most knew by heart: *Day is done; gone the sun, from the lake, from the hills, from the sky. All is well, safely rest, God is nigh.*

*****

Peggy Trickey remained with her mother-in-law in Berlin, following the funeral.

The two were widows, and Grace had lost her only son. They would attempt to be a comfort to each other through the difficult weeks ahead.

In the midst of the cold and gray days of late Wisconsin autumn, they had little Fred III to give their grieving hearts some respite, and there was something to look forward to with great hope--the birth of Colonel Trickey's second child.

It is likely that Peggy wanted that child to come into the world where his father had been born and had spent the golden years of his childhood and teens.

There, Peggy could feel her husband's vibrant presence still, in his old home, or driving by the school where he was the Big Man on Campus 13 years earlier. Many of his classmates had settled in Berlin, and perhaps helped ease the pain by sharing their pleasant memories of times past.

In a Berlin hospital on December 11, 1946, almost three months to the day after the bomber crash on Cold Mountain, Colonel Trickey's widow gave birth to their second son.

He was named Thomas Patrick Trickey, and was to be called by his middle name.

But little Patrick was born dead.

It was believed that the child, who was born a few weeks premature, did not survive because of Peggy's heart condition, and because of the stress she suffered following her husband's death on Cold Mountain.

Patrick's tiny body was buried beside Colonel Trickey's grave in the family plot in Berlin. The engraving on his stone reads simply *Thomas Patrick Trickey: 12-11-46: 12-11-46.*

The Trickey plot later became the burial spot of the Colonel's mother, who died on January 5, 1963, two days before her 85th birthday. And the site also contains the ashes of his sister, Dorothy Swetting Trickey, who died at age 72 in 1969. (After Dorothy's first marriage ended, she married a distant cousin, Paul Trickey.)

*****

COURAGEOUS PEG

Peggy Trickey mourned her husband and stillborn son, but did not waste precious time in self-pity.

She had little Fred III to raise and a life to live, and she knew that Colonel Trickey would want her to move on with the same courage and high spirit that had drawn him to her in the first place.

After spending time in Wisconsin after Patrick was stillborn, Peggy and her son returned to Tampa. They lived off base, but stayed in touch with friends stationed at MacDill Field and elsewhere.

Among those friends were Major Rod Francis and Major P.L. Yon, who remained close to the family throughout the years--and Major James Bratton Lampley, who served with Colonel Trickey in the 497th Bombardment Group and had been a pallbearer at his funeral.

In later years, Peggy Trickey explained to her son, "Major Lampley waited a respectable year before he came courting the Colonel's widow."

Fred Trickey III was three-years-old when his mother and Major Lampley exchanged wedding vows.

And after the Major was honorably discharged from the Air Force, the new little family unit moved to his native town--Hendersonville, North Carolina, which was less than 30 miles from Cold Mountain, "as the crow flies."

Colonel Trickey's son grew up in Hendersonville knowing his father had died in a bomber crash on a mountain "somewhere near Brevard," but during his youth he was never taken to the crash site nor did he seek to go.

Major James B. Lampley went into business with his father, James Hoyt Lampley, who was owner of the Chrysler-Plymouth auto dealership in Hendersonville.

Life was good--but one thing was missing. Peggy wanted to have a child with her second husband.

Doctors gave dire warnings about her heart condition and what might transpire if she attempted to bring another life into the world.

She might again face the heartbreak of having a stillborn child, and she was also putting her own life at risk. But she was determined to give it her best shot.

The last lines of the poem about brave men, which was read by Rev. Sneedsby at Colonel Trickey's funeral, could apply to Peggy Trickey Lampley as well: *What they have dared, they will dare again/Though they lose all else in the world beside.*

To the relief and joy of everyone, when Fred Trickey III was four-years-old, his mother introduced him to his healthy baby brother.

The new addition to the Lampley family was named James Clifford, for his father and paternal and maternal grandfathers. And he was called "Jimbo."

He was born in April of 1949, when the North Carolina mountains and valleys were turning green once more.

It was the April which would have been the fifth wedding anniversary for Peggy and Colonel Fred L. Trickey--but her happy second marriage and the birth of her second son kept T.S. Eliot's poem from being apropos that year.

The Lampley family was complete--and its two little boys would never consider themselves to be half-brothers.

Little Fred and Jimbo were brothers forever.

*****

ANOTHER HARSH TRANSITION

After having suffered such heavy blows in such a short period in 1946, Peggy Trickey Lampley had only a few blue-sky years before facing another.

Major James B. Lampley died of testicular cancer in March of 1954. He was only 36-years-old, and he and Peggy had been married less than six years.

Fred Trickey III was nine-years-old when his stepfather died, and his little brother was almost five.

Another grave far too soon made April of 1954, with its budding dogwoods and yellow daffodils nodding in the breeze, seem cruel indeed.

But again, the courageous Peggy held her head high and moved on, knowing that Major Lampley, like Colonel Trickey, would want her to do exactly that.

Now she had two small sons to raise alone--one who had no memory of his father, and one whose memory of his father would become vague with passing years.

*****

When Fred III was 10-years-old and his brother was six, Peggy took them on a trip to California, where they visited some of the people she had known when she was an Army Air Force wife.

"It's so terrible that you lost two husbands!" one woman lamented.

"I didn't *lose* my husbands," Peggy clarified with her usual humor and candor. "I lose gloves and earrings, but not husbands. They *died*."

Some wondered if she wouldn't marry again, since she was still young and attractive, and her sons needed a father. But Peggy's feeling was that she "had been married to two of the most wonderful men in the world," and could not ask for or expect more than that.

She remained single, and in an era when the insurance business was largely a man's domain, she became a licensed insurance broker and worked as such for many years.

*****

PEGGY'S BOYS GROW UP

After attending public elementary school in Hendersonville, Fred Trickey III completed his high school education at a private school, Christ School for Boys.

Christ School was located at Arden, N.C., a short distance from his home.

He made excellent grades and played basketball and soccer.

After graduating first in his class at Christ School, he entered the Honors Program at the University of North Carolina at Chapel Hill and studied under a Hap Arnold Scholarship, for students whose fathers died during the World War II period.

He majored in Math and Physics, but changed to English and Drama in his sophomore year. He had numerous roles with the renowned *Carolina Playmakers*, and considered pursuing a career as an actor.

After receiving his degree, he moved to New York City and worked in Columbia University Libraries for two or three years. while remaining interested in acting.

However, he soon developed another primary interest--in the astonishingly fast-growing field of computer technology.

And so Fred L. Trickey III, multi-gifted like his father, became a computer expert.

He was Information Security Officer at Columbia University for almost 20 years and was Regional Manager of Netigy Corporation from February, 2000 to March 2001.

In May 2001 he became the Information Security Administrator at Yeshiva University/Albert Einstein College of Medicine in New York City and was still in that post in 2005.

Fred L. Trickey's name is widely known in the Information Security field, and he is a frequent speaker at conferences throughout the United States and Europe.

He is an advisor to the Board of Directors for the New York Metro Chapter of ISSA (Information Systems Security Association) and a past president of the chapter.

He served on the Advisory Council of Computer Security Institute for three years, and was co-founder of a national forum, College and University Information Security Practitioners.

He has published magazine articles and chapters in handbooks on various topics related to Information Security.

Fred III has remained single, and he said, "I'm the last in my line of Trickeys."

In The Big Apple, he shares a home with his partner, Dr. Leigh Noble, who received a Ph.D in Mathematics from the University of Kentucky in December of 2004.

Fred's special interests include music, ranging from classical works from the 17th to 21st centuries to "classic rock" from the 1960s and 1970s; New York theatre, and gourmet cooking.

And he keeps in close touch with his brother "Jimbo"--who became famous.

*****

BROTHER JIM LAMPLEY

The son of Colonel Fred L. Trickey's widow and his good friend Major James B. Lampley attended public school in Hendersonville, and like Fred III, he enrolled at UNC-Chapel Hill after high school.

He studied under a Veterans Administration Scholarship for children of deceased World War II veterans.

And Peggy Trickey Lampley lived in Chapel Hill during the time her son was a student there.

For young Jim, a major break came in 1974, when he was in graduate school at UNC.

He was one of four chosen from 400 contestants in a nationwide talent search conducted by ABC-Television. The aim was to begin a program called *College Age Reporter*, for telecasts of college football.

After completing his graduate studies, the brother of Fred Trickey III spent three seasons with ABC, covering football in several states.

That set the stage for Jim Lampley's 13 years with ABC Sports--working football, baseball, Wide World of Sports, and Olympic games.

In 1987 he left ABC to work for CBS in Los Angeles and in the next five years he anchored 6 and 11 p.m. sports at KCBC-TV and was a sports correspondent for *CBS This Morning* in New York. He took over boxing and coverage of tennis at Wimbledon for HBO (Home Box Office Televison), hosted radio shows in New York and Los Angeles; and covered the Olympic games in Albertville.

Jim went to work for NBC Sports in 1992 and hosted NFL football for two years and anchored late night coverage of the Olympics in Barcelona and Atlanta.

In 1995, he added a magazine show, *Realsports*, to his duties at HBO, and has since won two Emmys for Best Sports Journalism and a third Emmy for writing.

In 1998, he anchored the Nagano Winter Olympics and the Goodwill Games for Turner Sports.

In 2004, he covered boxing for HBO, and was the daytime NBC anchor for the summer Olympics in Athens.

By then, he had been covering the Olympics over a period of 30 years, and he told sportswriter Caulton Tudor of the Raleigh *News & Observer* that the moment he remembered most was when the underdog American "miracle" hockey team beat the top-rated Soviets and won the Gold Medal in 1980 at Lake Placcid.

It was Jim Lampley's telephone that was passed around the locker room when President Jimmy Carter called to congratulate the players. "It was a madhouse, with everyone trying to get to the phone and celebrating at the same time," he recalled.

Jim Lampley has been married twice and has two sons and two daughters.

His second wife, the former Bree Walker, was a TV news anchor in Los Angeles when they met.

In 2004, Jim and Bree, who remained close following their divorce in 2000, appeared together with their son and daughter on the Larry King Live TV show to discuss the challenges Bree and the children face daily.

Bree, who is renowned for her work in promoting hiring of the handicapped, was born with a rare genetic disorder that caused her fingers and toes to be fused, or not developed beyond the first joint.

Doctors warned Bree and Jim of the strong chance that their children would inherit the same problem.

But Bree Walker-Lampley was as courageous and determined as her husband's mother, Peggy Trickey Lampley, had been when she took tremendous risks to bring him into the world.

The children of Jim and Bree-Walker Lampley were indeed born with the same problem as their mother, but they have faced their challenges with the same drive and spirit that made their grandmother, mother, father, and Uncle Fred so successful.

By 2005, Jim had homes in California and Utah, and was a successful restauranteur, along with his career as a sportscaster. And in 2006, he was an NBC anchor for the winter Olympics in Torino, Italy.

Fred L. Trickey III, left, enjoyed a visit with his nephew, Aaron Lampley, and brother Jim Lampley in Malibu in 2002.

The widow of the young hero pilot who died on Cold Mountain, and then widow of his good friend, surely became one of the proudest mothers in America. She had suffered great losses, fought the good fight, and raised two sons alone and prepared them to make their marks in the world.

Peggy Trickey Lampley's earthly task was completed on February 16, of 1985, after heart surgery in New York City. She made it through the operation, but died of pneumonia. She was 66 years old.

Among the first persons Fred III contacted about his mother's passing were Major Rod Francis and Major P.L. Yon, who had remained close to her and her sons throughout the years.

Having witnessed the anguish of loved ones of the deceased at traditional funerals, with or without an open casket, Peggy had requested that her body be cremated.

Her ashes were turned into the soil in Saint James Memorial Gardens in Hendersonville.

There, they became part of the ever-greening of spring.

*****

What would Lieuteant Colonel Fred Logan Trickey Jr. have thought of what happened after his death on Cold Mountain?

What would he have thought of his widow and son living in a town a short distance from the place he died?

What would he have thought of the son who carried his name and the son his Peg had with his old Army Air Force buddy?

The World War II hero who would not accept a *Silver Star* unless his entire bomber crew could receive the same honor, would no doubt have been pleased and proud of them all.

He would have flashed his captivating smile, and to Peggy Trickey Lampley, Fred L. Trickey III, Major James B. Lampley, and Jim Lampley, he likely would have said--"*WELL DONE!*"

*****

LIEUTENANT COLONEL
PAUL R. OKERBLOOM

A BOY CALLED "PETE"

Paul Richard Okerbloom, called "Pete" by family and friends, was born in Columbus, Ohio on September 16, 1915.

His father, Charles Irving Okerbloom, was a native of Stockholm, Sweden, and his mother, the former Huldah Anderson, was also of Swedish ancestry.

The couple began married life in Harrisburg, Pennsylvania, and were part of a tight-knit community made up of other Swedish immigrants. And those homeland ties remained strong when they moved to Ohio.

The Okerblooms and most of their neighbors were devout members of the Lutheran Church.

Charles I. Okerbloom was a traveling auditor for International Harvester Corporation, manufacturers of farm equipment. His profession put his family in the well-to-do category, and they had a summer home on the shores of Lake Erie, where the five Okerbloom children enjoyed swimming and boating.

Pete was the youngest of the five. His siblings were Vivian, Charles Jr., called "Chuck;" Dorothy, and Helen.

All the youngsters were bright and gifted, and Chuck and Dorothy exhibited artistic talent early in life.

Pete's inquisitive mind resulted in a more mechanical bent.

"He was a handsome young man with a great sense of humor--a real charmer," said Mary Clouser of Thelford Hill, Vermont, widow of Pete's nephew.

*****

SURPRISE!

When Pete Okerbloom was in his first year of an electrical engineering program at the University of Ohio, he was informed that he had received an appointment to West Point, the Army's renowned Military Academy in New York State.

His father, an Army enthusiast and member of the Ohio National Guard, had contacted an Ohio Congressman, who subsequently brought about the turn of events.

Pete knew nothing of the matter until he was told he was going to become a West Point Cadet.

He entered the Academy in July of 1935, and it was said that he was unprepared for, yet not dismayed by, the new and demanding route his life had taken.

At the picturesque and historic institution poised on a granite bluff above the Hudson River, young Okerbloom and his classmates and instructors soon learned that his keen interest in the new and unusual was well suited to Academy life.

It was said that during his four years at West Point, *"he neither startled the Academy nor received its frowns."* His grades were above average, and his extra-curricular activities included membership in the Camera Club, Radio Club, and Dialectic Club. He was also involved in numerous social activities, and *"in working on various gadgets that he kept as near to his room as tactical inspections would permit."*

*****

GOING TO THE CHAPEL

One Sunday during Plebe Year, young Okerbloom volunteered to show a few visitors through West Point's Cadet Chapel.

As a result, he was introduced to Marie Baer, daughter of Mr. and Mrs. Paul Baer of Mountain View, New Jersey--and a small spark between the pretty dark-haired girl and the dashing Cadet soon burst into flame.

Born on October 24, 1917, Marie was two years younger than Pete.

Pete graduated in June 1939, was assigned to the Signal Corps in the Army Air Corps, and was given a three-month leave.

During this leave, he and Marie Baer were married in the place where it all began—West Point Chapel. At the end of the ceremony, the beaming couple walked beneath a traditional canopy of swords held by the bridegroom's close friends.

Lieutenant Paul R. "Pete" Okerbloom and his bride, Marie, happily exited West Point Chapel in 1939.

In October of 1941, Lieutenant Okerbloom was transferred to Basic Training Flying School at Perrin Field at Sherman, Texas. This assignment lasted until August of 1943, and was the longest period that he and his beloved Marie were able to be together in one place.

He became Director of Training at Perrin Field and attained the rank of Major.

And he also became the proud and devoted father of a son, Paul Richard Okerbloom Jr., who was born on March 25, 1942.

The child's nickname was Dickie.

This snapshot of Major Okerbloom with Marie and their son, Dickie, was made in late 1942.

After undergoing pilot training in B-24 bombers at Fort Worth, Texas, Major Okerbloom was transferred to the Second Air Force and sent to the 15th Bomber Wing, headquartered at Gowen Field at Boise, Idaho.

At that time, the Second Air Force was installing a new aircraft maintenance system, known as Production Line Maintenance.

Major Okerbloom's previous experience with this system in the Air Training Command resulted in his assignment to the office of the Wing Air Inspector.

It was in this duty that he was promoted to Lieutenant Colonel.

Six months later, when the first B-29 bomber wings were being formed and trained for deployment, he became Air Inspector of the 73rd Bomber Wing at Colorado Springs, Colorado.

And the Wing was sent to the Pacific Theatre in October of 1944.

Prior to leaving for duty in the Pacific in 1944, Major Okerbloom shared special moments with little Dickie.

BROTHERS TOGETHER AGAIN

By 1944, Colonel Okerbloom's "big brother" Charles I. "Chuck" Okerbloom had become an enlisted man in the Army Air Force--and the two ended up at the same base on Saipan.

As Colonel Okerbloom flew bombing missions, his brother watched the mighty planes thunder off to an uncertain fate, and with great anxiety he counted them carefully as they returned to home base, praying all the while that Pete's plane would not be one that caused the total to come up short.

To keep his mind off the danger his brother faced, Chuck put his artistic talent to work decorating the mess hall. And when he finished, it was a much more cheerful and inviting place for the men to "chow down."

*****

After the War, Chuck Okerbloom became an Associate Professor of Art at Ohio State University, where he had graduated in 1930. And he later filled the same post at Tulsa University in Oklahoma.

The Colonel's brother was an accomplished cartoonist as well as a renowned painter, and he joined the Art Department at the University of Arkansas at Fayetteville in 1953, and attained a full professorship in 1963.

Professor Okerbloom was also an accomplished tennis player, and continued as such far into his senior years.

He retired in 1969, and died at age 91 in 1999, having been a renowned resident of the Fayetteville, Arkansas for 46 years.

In addition to the University of Arkansas, the works of Professor Charles I. Okerbloom Jr. are in collections and museums in Dallas, Texas; New Orleans, Louisiana; and Columbus and Toledo, Ohio. They are also in the permanent collection at Iowa State University.

It was his wish that an endowment of $100,000 would go to the University of Arkansas Art Department, to be used for scholarships, following his death. And that wish was fulfilled.

A MEDAL RECIPIENT

For his extraordinary service in the Pacific in World Was II, Colonel Paul R. Okerbloom was awarded the *Bronze Star* and *Air Medal.*

He was assigned to MacDill Field in Tampa in January of 1946, and was joined by the lovely girl from Mountain View, New Jersey, who less then six years earlier had begun a journey with him beneath a canopy of swords on the steps of West Point Chapel.

Also welcoming him to his new life in a nation at peace was little Dickie, who was almost four-years-old. It had been a long time since the child had had a chance to spend time with his father, and all three Okerblooms were looking forward to making up for lost time.

But only eight months later, their time as a family was frozen forever on Cold Mountain.

When Colonel Okerbloom's bright light was extinguished on The Mountain, waiting for him at MacDill Field were orders assigning him to Air National Guard duty in Chicago.

*****

A FRIEND REMEMBERS

The following tribute to the hero called Pete was gleaned from a 1948 West Point publication in memory of graduates who had died during or soon after the World War II period.

It was written by Colonel Okerbloom's former West Point buddy and classmate, Lieutenant Colonel Allen F. Herzberg.

His words are as follows:

Pete Okerbloom was a man who made friends readily, in diverse and seemingly odd directions. The thread that tied these friendships together was a mutual dislike of surface sham, coupled with an unassertive appreciation of individual worth.

Pete's humorous non-tolerance of convention and pride for its own sake made him a disconcerting puzzle to some, but to many more he was an interesting, wholehearted friend.

Those who knew him can only remember Pete as a succession of pleasant incidents. His absence leaves a void that makes the world a little duller, a little more circumscribed, a place from which some of the zest has gone.

His friends could, and did look forward to their next meeting with him. The closer one was to Pete the more essential he became to the true perspective and enjoyment of the ordinary foibles that make up life, if one can but see them.

This was his relation to his friends. To his family, an outsider can sense the relationship that existed, but any formulation in words can only be so inadequate as to be meaningless.

Pete was one of those rare catalysts who, to his friends, brought actuality out of the rhyme we all know:

"The world is so full of a number of things,
I am sure we should all be happy as kings"

Pete's interests were unlimited. Whether it was trying his hand at a lemon meringue pie, to the detriment of the kitchen, or the purchasing of an ancient slot machine to determine its mathematical probabilities, Pete was always an unpredictable step ahead.

To remember him is to smile as some incident comes to mind: a smile that becomes tinged with bitterness as one carries it into the present. The great gift of time is to be thanked that bitterness fades out, while the pleasant memories become more bouyant and sustaining.

Pete's friendship was as easy to wear as an old coat. His casualness, agreeability, and kindly yet penetrating comments, made him a welcome companion.

The depth of his convictions and emotions could only be gauged by his humorous disparagement when they were touched, and by lack of any action that would run counter to them.

He was all that is worthwhile and commendable. He was natural, human, enjoyed life deeply, and transmitted some of this spirit to those he touched.

This spirit remains undimmed.

*****

(Colonel Allen F. Herzberg outlived his remarkable West Point buddy by 59 years. At age 90, he died in Austin, Texas in 2003.)

When the B-25 bomber slammed into Cold Mountain, Colonel Okerbloom was only three days from his 31st birthday. Marie Okerbloom would mark her 29th birthday six weeks later.

Funeral services were held at West Point, with full military honors, and burial was in West Point Cemetery.

*****

NEW LIFE, NEW NAME

As time moved on, Paul Richard "Dickie" Okerbloom Jr. didn't remember much about his father or events prior to the bomber crash on Cold Mountain.

"I remember silly little things," he said, "such as having a party when the atom bomb was dropped on Japan and everybody knew the war was finally over."

And he had only a dim memory of the sad September day when his mother told him his father would not be coming home again.

Because he was at such a tender age, his mother thought it best that he not attend his father's funeral.

And shortly after the funeral, Marie and Dickie moved from Tampa to Mountain View, N.J. and lived with her parents for around four years.

Marie's father, Paul Baer, was a native of Switzerland and was an importer of Swiss lace. Her mother, Lucille, was also of Swiss ancestry.

Donald Baer, Marie's younger brother, was a wonderful surrogate father for Dickie while he lived in the Baer home.

After a time, Marie began work in New York City, as a secretary in the headquarters of the Sperry Rand Corporation, distributor of countless varieties of seeds and animal feeds that helped keep America's vast agricultural network flourishing.

In attaining her job, Marie had come to a new beginning, literally and symbolically. Sperry Rand seed products were the first step of a process that was often completed by the farm machines produced by International Harvester, the company that brought prosperity to the Okerbloom family in the days of her late husband's youth. The wheels of fate seemed to be coming full circle.

Winter was over, and it was time to plant the seeds for life's future harvest.

When Marie had been a widow for four years, and son Dickie was eight-years-old, she married again.

Her second husband had a last name that sounded similar to Okerbloom. He was Bert Tuttle Oakley, a Sperry Rand executive who had been Marie's boss.

But similarities between Bert Oakley and Colonel Okerbloom ended with the name. They were very different in looks and personality, and Bert Oakley had no military experience.

But he was a fine man and a devoted husband and father.

After the wedding, Marie and Dickie moved from New Jersey to their new home on Long Island, New York.

Marie didn't work outside her home after her second marriage.

All vacations were spent with the Baers in New Jersey. While Dickie was still young, he and his mother and stepfather visited his Okerbloom grandparents once in Ohio, and his Oakley step-grandparents once in Provo, Utah.

To some in the late 1940s, it might have been confusing that young Dickie's last name was Okerbloom, but his parents were Marie and Bert Oakley. But that had nothing to do with a change of Dickie's last name.

Bert Oakley adored his stepson, and wanted to be as much a real father to him as possible. His wish was to legally adopt the boy and give him his name.

Dickie was glad to have a father like the other boys his age, and when presented with the possibility of changing his last name to Oakley, it sounded like a fine idea.

And so the adoption was completed, and the first name, last name, and "junior" were dropped from Paul Richard Okerbloom Jr., and Dickie became simply Richard Oakley.

When Richard was 12-years-old, his mother gave birth to another son, Scott Oakley.

Scott was in first grade when Richard graduated from Wautagh High School on Long Island and was set to follow in the footsteps of his father.

He received an appointment to West Point.

"I was excited about going to West Point," Richard recalled. But after a time it became evident that he was not as cut out for the Academy as his father had been. And with the kind of frankness that Colonel Okerbloom would have admired, he explained, "I flunked out."

Richard was not as mechanically-minded as his father--but he had inherited a generous portion of talent from the artistic side of the Okerbloom family.

After leaving West Point, he enrolled in the School of Visual Arts in New York City.

*****

VISION ON A BLIND DATE

Outside his main area of studies, Richard Oakley's chief interests were soccer, music, and boating. And it was boating that created a lasting wave in his life.

During summer vacation after he entered The School of Visual Arts, Richard received a request from one of his friends from high school days. Would Richard take him and his girlfriend out on his boat?

And Richard's reply was, "I will if you'll get me a date."

He was a bit nervous about the blind date which his friend had arranged for an outing on Great South Bay. But when he met lovely dark-haired Joyce Ann Kali, he saw his future before him.

It was love at first sight.

Joyce, who was still in high school at the time, was the daughter of Anthony and Lydia Kali of Long Island. Her father was an attorney.

After high school graduation, Joyce completed studies leading to a career as a radiology technologist.

And after Richard received his degree from The School of Visual Arts, the couple exchanged wedding vows in a Catholic Church on Long Island. The wedding took place on June 4, 1966.

In time, the Oakley family expanded to include three sons and a daughter--Kurt Richard Oakley, Evan Scott Oakley, Megan Ann Oakely, and Bret Richard Oakley--the grandchildren of Lieutenant Colonel Paul R. Okerbloom.

From 1966 through 1970, Richard Oakley worked for independent designers in New York City, and then became a graphic designer for IBM at White Plains, New York.

The Oakleys lived in Connecticut for a time during his work with IBM.

One day in 1974, Richard's boss walked in with an easy question: "Who wants to go to Florida?" Richard's hand shot up immediately.

He was transferred to Boca Raton, and during the extended period that followed he accepted temporary assignments in Raleigh, North Carolina.

In April of 1984, Marie Baer Okerbloom Oakley died of lung cancer. She and her husband were living at Satellite Beach, Florida at that time.

Like Peggy, the widow of Lieutenant Colonel Fred L. Trickey Jr., Marie was 66-years-old at the time of her death.

AN OLD TRUNK TURNS BACK TIME

In years just after Colonel Oklerbloom's death in the bomber crash on Cold Mountain, his widow told young "Dickie" a lot about the remarkable man who was his father. But such memories sharpened the loss for Marie and caused her emotional pain.

And after she married again, the subject of the husband, father, and World War II hero called Pete was gently laid to rest.

So for many decades, the story of Richard Oakley's biological father lived only in pictures, the medals he had been awarded, the words written about him before and after his death, and one of his neatly folded uniforms--in a trunk that remained in the Baer home in New Jersey.

When Richard was still known as Dickie Okerbloom, and was around age six, he looked inside the trunk often and played with some of the contents, too young to fully comprehend their significance.

After the death of his grandparents, he inherited the trunk that held so many remnants of his father's too-brief time on earth.

When Richard began working in Raleigh, he got out the old trunk again and looked through it with a new perspective.

And in 1995, he felt an urge to go to the western part of the Tar Heel State and try to find someone who could tell him more about September 13, 1946 on Cold Mountain.

When he reached Haywood County, it didn't take long before he was directed to the Cruso home of O.C. Chambers, who decades earlier had helped his brother and friends roll a B-25 tire off the mountain.

O.C. shared his memories of the crash, and in turn Richard sent O.C. copies of papers that were in his father's trunk.

Richard was unable to go to the crash site at the time of his visit, but having talked with someone who had been to the spot soon after his father died, and being able to get a clear view of The Mountain, had satisfied a part of the son's longing.

And other contacts would be made in months to come.

In 2000, Richard Oakley retired in Boca Raton, and filled his free time with occasional design projects and part-time work at a local marina. And he continued to enjoy boating.

By 2005, his half-brother, Scott Oakley, who remained single, was living in Arizona and was an IT computer expert employed by the City of Phoenix.

Richard and Joyce Oakley's son, Kurt, was father of a daughter, Taylor, by his first marriage, and lived in Boca Raton with his second wife, Amy. He was an IT technician for Bell South.

Son Evan Oakley also lived in Boca Raton and was a professional musician, playing guitar and bass. Daughter Megan Oakley Johnson lived in South Florida with her husband, Ryan, and their daughter, Tate, and son, Jake.

And son Bret Oakley lived in Raleigh, where he worked as a computer programmer and had his own business designing Internet web sites.

Richard Oakley, the former Paul Richard "Dickie" Okerbloom Jr., and wife Joyce were pictured at their son's 2003 wedding.

At a 2003 wedding in Florida, three generations of descendants of Lieutenant Colonel Paul R. "Pete" Okerbloom were pictured, left to right, back--Ryan Johnson, Megan Oakley Johnson, granddaughter; Evan Oakley, grandson; Amy Oakley, Kurt's bride; Kurt Oakley, grandson; Mrs. Richard Oakley, Richard Oakley, son; Bret Oakley, grandson; and front--Tate Johnson, Jake Johnson, and Taylor Oakley, great-grandchildren.

Colonel Okerbloom would no doubt have been fascinated by the "new and unusual" twists and turns in the lives of his widow and small son following his death.

The man who lived his too-short life with deep love of family, joy of a brilliant mind, great humor, and heroic courage in America's darkest years of World War II would likely have been glad about how things turned out for those he left behind.

He would have been pleased that Richard Oakley, after losing contact with his Okerbloom aunts, uncle, and cousins for a time, established their relationship again, much to the delight of all.

The West Point graduate who "brought actuality" to the verse *"The world is so full of a number of things/ I am sure we should all be happy as kings,"* would have been happy, and at peace, in knowing what his son "Dickie" said when he was 62 years old--twice the age of his father when he died in the bomber crash on Cold Mountain.

Richard Oakley's words were, *"I'VE HAD A GREAT LIFE."*

*****

MASTER SERGEANT
HOSEY W. MERRITT

A BOY NAMED HOSEY

Hosey William Merritt was born on Route 1, Geneva, Alabama on August 13, 1918.

His parents were Charles R. and Ada Speigner Merritt, who were married in 1910.

His father, who was called "Charlie," was born in Union Springs in Bullock County, Alabama in 1886, and his mother was born in Dale County in 1880 and grew up in the County Line Baptist Church community five miles from Enterprise, Alabama, the Coffee County seat.

Hosey's father had little formal education, but he was a smart man and a hard worker, and he and Ada were better off than many residents of rural southeastern Alabama, because he had managed to buy a 40-acre farm a few miles from the tiny town of Coffee Springs.

On his property, Charlie built a two-bedroom white frame house, next to Eden Baptist Church, a little white church which later became a larger brick structure at the same site.

Samuel Quillar and Mrs. Clyde Justice of Geneva, Alabama remembered the Merritts well, and both said they were "some of the best people in the world."

On June 30, 1915, Charlie and Ada welcomed a son, Ramsey, into their home. And on the farm they had another arrival--which was not welcomed in any, way, shape or form.

It was in 1915 that the boll weevil destroyed cotton crops and left farmers without the profits they had depended on for decades. Likewise, it left merchants without many rural customers who had been their life-blood for years.

But after a short time, farmers learned that there was money to be made through growing peanuts instead of cotton. Peanuts replenished the soil that years of cotton had depleted of nutrients, and the really good part was that the boll weevil had no appetite for peanuts and moved on to other cotton fields in other places.

Farmers in southeastern Alabama again had money in their pockets, and merchants again heard their cash registers go "ding" many times during harvest season.

Peanuts had saved the area's economy and a celebration was in order.

In the main business district of Enterprise, a tall statue of a lady in a gracefully flowing gown was erected in 1919, the year after Hosey Merritt was born. It was a tribute to a new day of prosperity.

The statue, which some people thought looked a lot like the Lady Liberty (the Statue of Liberty) held her arms high, and in her hands was a refreshing fountain with waters which cascaded over her head.

The statue was made in Italy, and cost a small fortune. But a statue like that might have been in any town, anywhere. Did it really give a message about the terrible time that had befallen the area and how it had flourished again?

Why not have the lovely statue lady hoist a huge peanut over her head?

A prominent citizen didn't think much of that idea, and convinced others that the statue needed to pay tribute to the basic root of their better days--namely the lowly and evil boll weevil that had forced farmers to grow peanuts.

Out of something bad had come something good! When the soil was nourished once more, and the boll weevil had moved on, cotton could be grown again, along with peanuts.

And so the lady's high fountain, which had been destroyed by vandals anyway, was replaced by a giant boll weevil.

Now that was a statue like none other in the world--one that paid tribute to a pesky insect--and the news media eventually spread its story far and wide. The "Bug Lady" became famous, and Enterprise, Alabama was on the map of places to visit and unusual things to see in the sunny South.

Through the years, the statue went through extremely hard times, just like the farmers who had been devastated by the boll weevil. Among many disasters befalling the beautiful lady and her big pest was being toppled and buried in a shallow grave by several teenage boys in search of something exciting to do in the summer of 1948.

In 2005, the statue was still standing proudly on the town square and drawing large numbers of tourists. And it was protected by a sophisticated security alarm system.

*****

FARM LIFE NOT FOR HOSEY

No one knows what Hosey Merritt thought of the boll weevil statue when he became old enough to see it in his neighboring county and learn of its history. But one thing was certain when he grew into his teen years—be it cotton or be it peanuts—he had no interest in becoming a farmer.

He knew of the hardships that came with the Great Depression of the early 1930s, and he wanted a future with more promise and less grueling labor than agriculture could offer.

When something needed doing on the Merritt farm, young Hosey usually came up with something else "important" to do, and the chores fell to his brother Ramsey.

Ramsey felt a closer connection to the Alabama soil and its profitable products, and he spent much of his adult life as an employee of the Geneva Cotton Mills. He was a mechanic who kept the machinery in working order.

Hosey's primary interest lay in the wonders of technology that had just begun to surface in rural areas of the South in the 1930s.

The section where his family lived did not have electricity until late in 1946, and until around that same time the Merritts' only mode of transportation was a horse.

However, the world was brought to their doorstep through a battery radio. And it was radio and how it worked that captivated young Hosey's imagination.

He was an excellent student at Hartford High School, but his teachers couldn't tell him all he wanted to know about radio and how it could be possible to turn a knob and hear music and someone talking from hundreds of miles away.

When Hosey was 15-years-old, he was reading a magazine when a special advertisement caught his eye. He learned he could send off some money and take a correspondence course in radio.

The prospect was too exciting to pass up, and so Hosey came up with the fee and completed the course.

He was a boy who believed in reaching for the heights, and felt that others should do the same, one way or other.

His nephew, Jerry Merritt of Eufaula, Alabama, who was born in 1941, remembers his uncle holding him high over his head and teaching him to "walk on the ceiling."

Hosey's brother and his wife, the former Esther Bryan, also had two daughters, Mary Ellen, who was born in 1939; and Janice Marie, who was born in 1945.

Esther said Hosey ate at their house often, and she enjoyed cooking for him.

He was a good-looking young man, around 5' 9'' tall with brown hair and blue eyes. His face reflected his intelligence and sensitivity, and unlike typical images of a shy farm boy, he was flamboyant and a dapper dresser.

He had an eye for pretty girls, and many a young lady responded to his admiring glances.

In addition to his interest in radio and other intriguing aspects of science, Hosey had artistic talent. One of his nephew's keepsakes is a sling-shot handle on which his uncle drew an excellent picture of a bathing beauty.

By the time he was 17, Hosey was "chomping at the bit" to see the world beyond Geneva and Enterprise and the wide stretches of farmland in between.

He was a junior at Hartford High School when his yearning for independence and adventure grew so strong that he left his studies and joined the military.

It was a common occurance among young men at that time.

*****

AHEAD OF THE GAME

Hosey's early course in radio put him a jump ahead when he entered the Army Air Force in the mid-1930s.

After basic training, the boy who grew up with a horse as his family's chief mode of transportation, was flying high as radio operator on some of America's most sophisticated military aircraft.

At first, he was part of a light bombardment group flying coastal anti-submarine patrol missions to protect America's shipping interests in the Caribbean. A few years later, he was assigned to medium bombers, including the A-20 "Havoc," which was developed in the late 1930s and known as the DB-7. The aircraft was first used by France in a 1940 bombing attack on Germany.

Sergeant Merritt, left, and a fellow crew member are pictured with a DB-7/A-20 "Havoc."

The Sergeant's commanding officer was Colonel Lloyd H. Watnee, whose nickname was "Jiggs."

And at an unspecified date, Sergeant Merritt was among 13 men who received the *Air Medal* for outstanding service.

It was written that the men were *honored for their long and continued service in the performance of hazardous duties on anti-submarine patrol when their unit flew hundreds of routine sweeps and missions in ending the submarine menace to our shipping in the Caribbean area.*

It was noted that, in one month alone, they chalked up 1,141 flying hours in only 10 patrol planes.

When the outfit returned to the United States, it was largely broken up, with many men assigned to other squadrons.

However, Sergeant Merritt and the 12 others remained with Colonel Watnee at Mountain Home Army Air Base in Idaho, where they were a training nucleus for a new heavy bombardment outfit.

The article reporting the assignment stated: *Each man considers his present heavy bomber assignment the most important of his long bombing career.*

*****

HOSEY'S WOMEN

Anyone looking for Sergeant Hosey W. Merritt in his off-duty hours would likely find him in the company of a good-looking woman.

His ability to charm members of the opposite sex, that he demonstated so well in his teen years, increased abundantly when he joined the Army Air Force.

He was a natural "ladies' man," and wearing a uniform only added fuel to the fires that he was so skilled at setting.

Sergeant Hosey Merritt could often be found with a pretty woman. The one in this photo is unidentifed--but the cigarettes on the table are Lucky Strikes.

By 1943, the farm boy from Alabama was down South once more, and in love with a dark-haired beauty from Savannah, Georgia. Her name was Mary Burns.

The two exchanged wedding vows on July 24, 1943 in Jacksonville, Florida.

Sergeant and Mrs. Hosey W. Merritt posed for this portrait at the time of their 1943 wedding.

The Sergeant's bride came to the Merritt farm in Alabama to get to know her in-laws, and it was a pleasant time for all. She posed for husband's camera while perched atop peanut haystack and on his family's horse.

The new Mrs. Hosey W. Merritt got acquainted, somewhat tentatively, with the horse that had been the Merrit family's chief mode of transportation for many years.

No one knows exactly what caused their breakup, but the marriage of the Sergeant and the girl from Savannah ended after a couple of years.

After he died on Cold Mountain, his death certificate listed him as "single." But those who knew him best knew that he would not have been without a lady in his life--and the evidence was published far from his Alabama home.

He was the subject of an item in the newspaper in Berlin, Wisconsin --hometown of Lieutenant Colonel Fred L. Trickey Jr.

The Berlin paper carried large front page stories about Colonel Trickey, his heroic career, and tragic death. And a day or so later it ran another front page item stating that *"Helen Cismoski of Spring Lake (near Berlin) was a close friend of M/Sgt. Hosey Merritt, who died with Col. Trickey and the three others in the B-25 bomber crash."*

(In 1946, it is likely that the news media would have used the term "close friend" to describe a relationship that was somewhat more than that.)

Did Colonel Trickey introduce Sergeant Merritt to one of his friends in Wisconsin? A girl named Genevieve Cismoski was a classmate of the Colonel's in Berlin High School.

Or was the connection only an irony further linking the men who died on Cold Mountain?

Sergeant Merritt's watch, which had stopped at 11:30 a.m. on the day of the bomber crash, was sent to his family by military officials.

He had celebrated his 28th birthday exactly one month before the crash.

News stories noted that Sergeant Merritt was the bomber's radio operator, and some reports also listed him as crew chief.

*****

HOME TO THE FARM

When the Sergeant's remains were returned to the farm house in rural Alabama, two servicemen accompanied the coffin and took turns standing guard around the clock for two days and two nights.

His devastated parents wanted to open the casket and have one last look at their son, but as in the case of the others who died in the crash, the guards could not allow it.

B.D. "Buck" Driggers, Charlie Merritt's best friend, sat up all night with him after the awful news about his son had come from North Carolina.

And when word spread, a large number of friends, relatives, and neighbors came to the house to express their sympathies.

The funeral, with military rites, was held in County Line Baptist Church and burial was in the church cemetery. (The church is in Coffee County and the cemetery is in Dale County, hence the name.)

The two servicemen who accompanied the coffin remained until the funeral was over.

*****

A UNIQUE TOMBSTONE

Jerry Merritt was only five-years-old when his Uncle Hosey died on Cold Mountain, but he remembers his funeral well. The men in their Army uniforms, the shots of their rifles that split the late summer air, and the Flag-draped coffin were all sealed in his mind forever.

Sergeant Merritt's niece, Janice Merritt Bush of Eufaula, inherited the Flag that draped his coffin, and will pass it on to her son, John Bush.

Like Fred L. Trickey III, Jerry Merritt is the last to carry the Merritt surname in his family line--but it lives on in other ways.

John Bush is a published poet whose pen name is "John Merritt," and Jerry's granddaughter is Sarah Merritt Hansen, daughter of Jerry's daughter Jennifer, and son-in-law, Dr. Todd Hansen.

The Hansens reside in Gastonia, North Carolina, where Dr. Hansen is a family physician.

Charlie Merritt was 60-years-old when his son died on Cold Mountain. He was never a man with money to spare--but he and his wife were determined that Hosey would have a fine monument on his grave--regardless of the cost.

Their hearts were broken, but they still held all the compassion that any hearts could hold--and Charlie and Ada wanted to put the names of the four men who died with Hosey on his tombstone.

And so the monument in County Line Baptist Church Cemetery is, in its special way, as rare as the famous statue which stands five miles away in Enterprise.

There is no tombstone like it anywhere else in the world.

A standing stone is inscribed MERRITT and beneath it is a six-foot long flat stone engraved with the image of a B-25 bomber at the top. Underneath that is: M/Sgt. Hosey William Merritt: born Aug. 13, 1918; died in crash of B-25 bomber on Cold Mountain, N.C. Sept. 13, 1946.

Below that inscription is an American Flag, and below the Flag are the words: In Memorium to Others Who Gave Their Lives: Maj. Gen. Paul B. Wurtsmith, Lt. Col. Fred L. Trickey, Lt. Col. P.R. Okerbloom, S/Sgt. Hoyt W. Crump.

The boy who couldn't be kept down on the farm became the hero who, in a symbolic way, brought his heroic bomber comrades home with him to stay--home where their names would remain in the serene Alabama countryside, surrounded by the warmth and caring that has long typified residents of that area.

This photo shows the top of the monument on the grave of Sergeant Hosey W. Merritt.

This is the bottom part of the monument on Sergeant Merritt's grave. (Both photos are courtesy of Gail Speigner of Enterprise, AL.)

(The Merritt gravesite can be reached by taking Highway 167 south from Enterprise four or five miles, then turning left on Highway 92 and going one more mile. County Line Baptist Church and Cemetery are on the righthand side of the road.)

*****

THE GENERAL'S LADY WRITES

Among the items kept by the Merritt family through the years is a letter to Hosey's mother from Irene Wurtsmith, wife of Major General Paul B. Wurtsmith.
It reads as follows:

1561 Roslyn Road
Grosse Pointe, Mich.
15 Dec. 1946

Dear Mrs. Merritt:

I know words at this time are very futile, but I want you to know that I know of the sorrow you are going through with the loss of your son, M/Sgt. Merritt.

There hasn't been a day that I haven't thought about all who were in the fatal plane in which my husband, General Wurtsmith, was also a passenger.

If at any time I can be of any help to you I would be more than pleased to do so, as I know that in sharing our common sorrow we can be a great comfort to each other.

Yours very sincerely,

Mrs. Paul B. Wurtsmith

The address indicates that, at the time, Mrs. Wurtsmith was staying with, or visiting, General Wurtsmith's brother, Dr. Ferdinand L. Wurtsmith, and his family.

The General's widow continued to send Christmas cards to the Merritt family for a number of years.

*****

ANOTHER TRAGIC LOSS

On February 4, 1954, Charlie and Ada Merritt lost their other son, Ramsey, at age 38.

His widow, Esther Merritt Payne of Dothan, Alabama, said his death was caused by a blood clot which formed in his leg and moved to his lungs.

Hosey's nephews and nieces were 14, 13, and 9 years old when their father died.

During the War, Hosey kept a photo album tracing his military career, the places he had been, and the people he had known for a long time or just a little while. And pictures of his nephew and nieces had prominent spots in his album.

Having no children of his own, the Sergeant had treasured Jerry, Mary, and Janice. And he unknowingly passed his artistic talent on to them.

Jerry Merritt spent a number of years working for advertising firms in Atlanta and Birmingham, and then became a professional artist specializing in paintings of historic sites and buildings, with a studio at his home near Lake Eufaula.

His sister, Mary Merritt Heinemann, who lives nearby, is a retired registered nurse and an amateur artist who exhibits at various shows, and his sister Janice Merritt Bush of Abbeville, Alabama is an accomplished photographer.

Jerry's second wife, Kay, is also a professional artist.

Sergeant Hosey Merritt would probably have been pleased to know that he and Lieutenant Colonel Paul R. Okerbloom would have something in common beyond being on the same plane in mid-September of 1946.

(Colonel Okerbloom's brother was an art professor, his sister was an amateur artist, and his son became a graphic designer.)

Kay Merritt is a native of Michigan, and her sister lived at Mount Clemmons near Detroit, which was home of Selfridge Air Force Base, where General Paul B. Wurtsmith was stationed for a time and the place from which the B-25's doomed flight began on September 13, 1946.

And Kay's sister had a summer home at Oscoda, where Wurtsmith Air Force Base was located.

Kay had seen the base many times, but never dreamed she would marry a man from Alabama whose uncle died on the plane with the man for whom Wurtsmith Air Force Base was named.

"I had a very strange feeling when I saw General Wurtsmith's name on Uncle Hosey's grave," Kay said.

*****

Sergeant Merritt's mother, Ada, died at age 85 on February 1, 1965.

Her tombstone in County Line Baptist Church Cemetery tells that she was *"separated by death"* from her husband Charlie and is now *"Resting Eternally Above with Her Children."*

Charlie Merritt was nearly six years younger than Ada, and they had been married for 55 years when he became a widower.

In future years, he moved his house from his farm to a lot in Geneva. And moved it another time also.

"Granddaddy could have built another house cheaper than moving the old one," Jerry Merritt said. "But he probably wanted to hang onto it for sentimental reasons."

It was the house where his two sons were born and grew up, and where Hosey's remains rested for two days, and two nights in the soft glow of lamplight in September, 1946.

*****

A COLORFUL LIFE

Sergeant Merritt's father had suffered great losses, and if he could have given his years on earth to his two sons whose lives were cut so short, he would have gladly done so. But since that was not possible, he chose to live each of his days to the fullest, and he remained as strong and enduring as the Alabama fields he tended in his younger years.

Affectionately called "Uncle Charlie" by citizens of his area, he was a colorful character in more ways than one.

He always kept a lot of hunting dogs, and would tell folks he had gotten rid of most of them, and then add, "I'm down to my best ten now."

After he installed the gravestone honoring his son and the other men who died on Cold Mountain, Charlie decided to paint the base of the standing Merritt monument a "grass green."

He wanted to give it some color amid the clay and gravel in the church cemetery. "Granddaddy thought it looked good," Jerry Merritt said, "but it actually looked awful."

Years later, Jerry and Kay removed the paint from the stone base and have maintained the graves in the Merritt plot since then.

A while after Charlie Merritt became a widower, it became obvious that Hosey's penchant for the ladies had been inherited.

In his early 80s, Charlie took a shine to a young woman, a college-age friend of the family who sat with him on his front porch swing one pleasant afternoon and complimented him on his good looks and sharp mind.

And as a result of his late-life "crush," Charlie went on a special shopping trip to town one day.

Jerry Merritt said he almost fell over the next time he saw his grandfather, and he gasped, "Granddaddy! What on earth have you done!?"

What Charlie had done was dye his hair a "Carrot Top" red. And his reply to his grandson's question was, "I did it myself! How do you like it?"

Jerry said he had to sit his grandfather down and convince him that it didn't look as good as his natural gray, and also make him realize that it was not a very good idea to be getting romantic notions about a woman who was young enough to be his granddaughter.

So Charlie got back on a more logical track with his hair color and love life, and married Myrtle Pritchett, who was only 20 years his junior.

In his old age, Charlie ate a big breakfast to begin each day, and a big meal at noon--and after his late evening walk he ate nothing but cornbread and buttermilk--topped off by whiskey-soaked ginseng root and two shots of whiskey, no more, no less.

He was well on his way to age 97, and still going strong, when he died on November 12, 1982.

In County Line Church Cemetery, his grave is near that of his first wife, Ada, their two sons, and the memorial he established for all the men who died on Cold Mountain.

Sergeant Hosey W. Merritt knew firsthand the miracle of radio, and in his short time on earth may have come to know it as only one of myriad miracles that people can encounter every day, if they will only recognize them for what they are.

Kay Merritt said, *"THE FAMILY FEELS THAT UNCLE HOSEY'S SPIRIT IS STILL VERY MUCH WITH US."*

And who can say that it was not Hosey's spirit that helped his father live such a long and colorful life?

*****

STAFF SERGEANT
HOYT W. CRUMP

From Hoyt - Spring 1943

A BOY NAMED HOYT

Hoyt Woodrow Crump was born on November 26, 1918 in the rural Reed Creek area of Hart County in northeastern Georgia.

The oldest of seven children, his parents were Dessie Inez Ayers and Perry O. Crump. When the couple married in early 1918, Perry was 22-years-old and Dessie was still in her teens.

Perry's father had been a storekeeper, but he had so many children that he felt he couldn't pass his business on to any of them. So Perry became a tenant farmer and sharecropper, and it was a hard-scrabble life for him and his young family.

In 1919, Perry and Dessie Crump posed for a portrait with little Hoyt, the first of their seven children.

Hoyt's four brothers and two sisters and years of birth were: Mack, 1920; Alton, 1922; Audrey, 1925; Jack, 1928; Wayne, 1933; and Jan, 1936.

In this 1933 snapshot, 14-year-old Hoyt Crump, left, holds baby brother Wayne, and his other siblings are, left to right: Mack, Alton, Audrey, and Jack.. (Sister Jan would arrive later.)

Like the rural Alabama home of Sergeant Hosey W. Merritt, there was no electricity at the Crump residence when the children were growing up, and therefore no indoor plumbing or "conveniences" of any kind.

Hoyt's father had only a sixth grade education. He enjoyed reading newspapers and magazines in his precious minutes of spare time, but now and then had to have his wife and children help him with the words.

After completing the eighth grade at Reed Creek School, young Hoyt had to drop out.

The nearest high school was in Hartwell, 12 long miles down the dusty dirt road from his home. There were no school buses coming his way, and the Crumps had no car or other means to transport him back and forth to classes.

Youngsters living in that rural Georgia area at the time had to room with someone near a high school if they had any hope of receiving a diploma.

Perry Crump didn't mind too much that his oldest son had quit school after eighth grade. After all, he had received more years of education than his father, and even more important was the fact that Hoyt's help was needed on the farm.

Hoyt was a good worker, and he gained a reputation for being able to pick more cotton, faster and longer, than anyone in Hart County.

He was a lanky youngster with long fingers that could pluck the cotton from the prickly bolls without getting his fingers scratched or the soft white puffs snared.

*****

DESSIE CRUMP'S DREAM

It was all well and good that young Hoyt Crump was a fine farm hand, but that didn't keep something from weighing heavily on his mother's heart and mind.

Dessie Crump was well aware, as were many others, that Hoyt was a very intelligent lad. From their point of view, it was a shame that he had to end his education when there might be a bright future waiting for him beyond Georgia's sun-baked fields.

Hoyt's mother was a devout Christian, a strong Baptist woman who was considered an absolute saint by members of her church and community. In spite of all she had to do to take care of her house and children and help in other ways on the farm, she made time to visit the sick and carry food wherever needed. In times of trouble and sorrow, Dessie was there to listen with a sympathetic ear and comfort through sharing her strong faith.

It was said that Dessie was the "soul" of the Crump family. She was quietly steady with whatever project she was working on, and always finished as planned.

On the otherhand, her husband Perry was the "backbone" of the family, a pragmatic man who labored almost non-stop to keep his family afloat.

Perry Crump wasn't inclined to attend church every Sunday with his wife. He said Jesus was good, but he didn't have much use for preachers of the Gospel, or other professionals, who had never gotten their hands dirty, had never had sweat pouring from their brows, and in fact didn't know the meaning of hard work.

Perry said he knew what kind of people had formed the great United States of America--and had kept it strong through the years. Farmers and others who bowed their backs and hoisted the heaviest loads had also hoisted Old Glory on high, and those who sacrificed with military service in times of war had kept it waving proudly in the breeze.

In the late 1930's, nationally syndicated writer Harold Martin wrote about the Crump family's hard struggles, and how they had a reversal of fortune.

When President Franklin D. Roosevelt took office in 1932, the country was on its knees, with the jack-booted foot of the Great Depression pressing on its neck.

Roosevelt's "New Deal" ushered in many programs that put Americans back to work and offered help to those deemed worthy of such. And Perry Crump became a grateful beneficiary of one of those programs--through the Farm Security Administration (FSA).

Harold Martin's story, about the Crump family and the FSA (published in 1939) is, in part, as follows:

HOW PERRY CRUMP
GOT A PIECE OF LAND

Up in Washington, D.C., Congress, spurred on by big operators in their home communities who fight FSA because it is slowly chipping away at the old sharecropper system, remember the old days when FSA was lavish with loans and outright grants.

So they crack the whip over it, placing on greater restrictions--which is a good thing up to a certain point, because it weeds out of FSA policy the things that were unsound.

But there is a danger that FSA will get too tough, and will cease to be what it has been--a helping hand to the man who is worthy of help.

One of the bright spots in FSA's record in Hart County, Georgia, for instance, is what Perry Crump has done in the Nancy Hart District.

Perry Crump was a tenant farmer.

When he got married in 1918, he went out with one mule and his plow gear to make a living, having in mind the dream of some day owning land of his own.

He got along pretty well for a few years. He held his own, but he didn't get close to his dream.

Then in 1925-26, the great drought struck. Perry Crump saw his cotton seed lie dead in the ground for lack of water. He saw his corn wither and turn yellow.

He came to the end of 1926 owing $400, with not a dime to pay his debts. (By that time his son Hoyt was eight years old, and there were three other young mouths to feed.)

Perry Crump sold his mule to have a little money to run on, and he slid back down the ladder a step.

As a tenant farmer, he could pretty well farm as he pleased, paying his standing rent. But as a sharecropper he had to farm like the landowner wanted him to.

By living so hard that even now he hates to think of it, he made enough to pay off his debts.

It took him seven years to get enough ahead to buy himself another mule and take that long step up the ladder to being a tenant farmer again.

In 1935, he did pretty well and got his mule paid for.

And in 1936 he was able to buy another mule, so that his son, Hoyt, then 17, could help him in the fields.

He knocked along for three years, doing fairly well, but still nowhere near being in shape to buy a farm of his own. He was always working the other man's land.

Then one day a letter came.

It said that any tenant farmer interested in buying a farm for himself should send in an application in to the FSA office in Hartwell.

Perry Crump sat down and filled in the application. He told what he had been able to do, and what he wanted to do.

After he mailed in his application, many days passed and no reply was received.

So he just forgot about it. To him, it didn't seem real anyway.

Then one afternoon when Perry was planting corn, three men drove up. They were Frank Seawright, Erskine Sadler, and George Deane, members of the FSA committee.

And they had news.

Perry Crump's FSA application had been approved by them, and they were of the opinion that the Government would loan him the money to buy a farm!

Perry didn't sleep a wink that night, and neither did his wife. They just lay awake talking about the chance to buy land of their own, and how they could make it blossom like a rose--if they could only get the loan.

And so it was that the FSA loaned Perry Crump $3,000 to buy 108 acres in the Cedar Creek area of the Nancy Hart District of Hart County, and another $1,000 for improvements. He had 40 years to pay it all off.

He got a good piece of land. It was rundown land, but Perry knew what to do with it. And what he didn't know, the Agriculture Extension Service man, the Conservation man, and the FSA unit supervisor could tell him.

Now, (late 1930s) Perry Crump's farm is one of the prettiest in Hart County.

He is getting away from cotton. In his hardest years, he held onto his one cow, and his wife and children lived off its milk and butter. Now he is going in for dairy cattle. He is building himself a nice dairy barn out of the profits he has made on his land. He has not missed a payment on his FSA notes.

He also went in with 11 other farmers to borrow more money to buy tractors and tillers and a seed cleaner and a combine, in an Association they call the Nancy Hart Feed and Seed Association.

And the Association is paying off its note on the dot.

When Perry Crump gets his place improved like he wants it, he can become a Grade A dairy farmer instead of Grade B.

If he keeps his health and the seasons are halfway right, he can pay off his $4,000 long before the 40 years are up.

Critics of the FSA think the deadwood has to be weeded out--the 100 who couldn't make it, some of them just because they were sorry. And you can never subsidize sorriness.

And some of them failed because a too-generous government got them into water over their heads.

But the fear is, that in trying to guard against failures such as these, they may bar the door to the many deserving ones who would not fail if given a chance.

Jimmy Maxwell, the local FSA unit supervisor, who is conservative by nature, said, "It was a good thing when we quit giving a man more than he could carry--but it will be bad if we get to the point where we don't give him enough to make it."

*****

ANOTHER MULE NOT ENOUGH

A short time before Perry Crump landed his FSA loan, there were rumblings in the air that didn't set too well with him.

As Harold Martin pointed out in his article, Perry had been fortunate enough to buy another mule in 1936. He and his son Hoyt were getting twice as much work done in the fields.

But now Perry was hearing folks say that it was time for Hoyt to get back in school and earn a high school diploma. His brothers were big enough to help their Daddy on the farm.

It had been around five years since Hoyt had left school after eighth grade, and his father couldn't see any reason he should return to the restraints of the classroom. What good would it do him to go back now?

Why, Hoyt was older than his mother when she got married, older even than his mother was when he was born! He could make a good life for himself right there on the farm.

But Dessie Crump was determined that her son would have an education--and she gained a strong ally on her side.

As fate would have it, Dessie's partner in the continuing education project was the pastor of Reed Creek Baptist Church.

It is not known if that preacher had learned the vital life lesson of hard labor, or if Perry warmed up to him in a significant way, but it really didn't matter much. The divine combination of a mighty good wife and mother and a man who stood behind a Bible and pulpit on Sundays was just too much to go up against.

So Perry Crump relented and agreed to let his finest farm hand go back to school.

The minister provided the Crumps information about the Martha Berry School for Boys near Rome, Georgia. At the time, it was commonly known as "the school for poor boys."

It was a boarding school, and all students had to help support the institution by working on the school's farm, which was right up Hoyt's alley. Martha Berry also included a girls school and small college.

Hoyt's application was submitted. And the news soon came that he had been accepted to begin his freshman high school year at age 18.

He made excellent grades at the Berry School, and was a member of the board of the Athenian Literary Society and a star on the school's track team.

One day, students from the school were riding in the backs of three large trucks, headed to town and a rare treat of a picture show.

The truck on which Hoyt was riding veered onto a soft shoulder of the road and overturned.

Fearing his family had heard the news on the radio, he penned a quick letter explaining what had happened.

It was the first of many letters illustrating that Hoyt Crump's major worry throughout his life was that his loved ones would worry about him. The following, transcribed in part, is one of several letters that seemed to be "prophetic" in nature--when read after September 13, 1946.

There were about forty boys on the truck I was on. All of us were thrown out, and several hit a pine tree. Two were killed instantly, and several had broken legs or arms.

I was thrown clear of the trees, so wasn't hurt, but just shaken up. I got one of the boys out and he was dead, because I felt of his heart and it wasn't beating. I couldn't tell who he was because his head was all busted up. He was bleeding from his mouth and ears, and my clothes were covered all over in his blood.

I know I never will forget how he looked.

Five of the boys are still in Rome Hospital, and several are limping this morning. It sure was terrible. All are good friends of mine and I hope they get well.

Remember, don't worry about me because I am perfectly O.K. Tell Mack and Harold and Doyle that I may sound too grown up--but for God sake to stop driving reckless! Once you live through a wreck like I have you will know better than to do it. Of course wrecks happen to the best of drivers, but it pays to be careful.

Write when you have time,

Love, Hoyt

In his last year at Martha Berry School, 1939-40, Hoyt received first prize for his senior essay on the topic of the importance of the campus as a bird sanctuary. It was neatly typed and without a single error.

It concluded: *Most of the campuses of our country have suffered from formal landscaping. This type of campus makes it almost impossible for birds to find food and refuge. On this type of campus well-like hedges, triangular shrubs, closely cropped circles, and hole-eliminating activities of the tree surgeon have almost spoiled the school grounds for birds.*

Berry has done much to make the campus grounds of the different schools attractive for the birds. First, the campus is kept as natural as possible, and protection is afforded against the natural enemies of birds. Second, bird houses, feeding stations, bird baths, and lakes have been established over the grounds for safety and conveniences of birds. And third, the students of Berry know and appreciate the economic as well as aesthetic value of birds to mankind.

Hoyt received his high school diploma at age 21. By then, Hitler's Nazi forces had invaded Poland and America was in the throes of "war jitters." Would the United States be drawn into war? No one could be certain about what lay ahead.

What would be Hoyt's future? He might have continued college at the Berry School--but at the time it seemed a better idea to join the Army Air Force. (After 1939, the official name was changed to Army Air Force, but many still referred to it as Air Corps.) .

Around the same time, Hoyt's brother, Mack Crump, enlisted in the Navy.

(Mack's nicknames were "Pinkie" and "Red." He was the only one of the five Crump boys with copper-colored hair and light freckles. The others shared their mother Dessie's Cherokee heritage and were dark-haired and with skin that tanned to very dark in the sun.)

After basic training in the Casey Jones School of Aeronautics at Newark, N.J., Hoyt was assigned to an anti-submarine patrol unit at Borinquen Field at San Juan, Puerto Rico.

In this early time of service he was an airplane engine mechanic, and later became a flight engineer on planes searching for enemy submarines in the Caribbean.

*****

BROTHER AT PEARL HARBOR

Hoyt's brother Mack was serving at Pearl Harbor when it was bombed by the Japanese on December 7, 1941. He was one of the fortunate ones who lived through it.

It was a horrible time for the entire country. The Pearl Harbor death toll was over 2,400, and America was plunged into the War against Germany and Japan.

The following is the letter Hoyt wrote the day after the attack on Pearl Harbor.

Monday night
December 8, 1941

Dear Mom and All,

I just received your letter yesterday, right after I heard about the Pearl Harbor bombing. I can't tell you how sorry I am that you didn't get my letters, because I did write them. Maybe you will get them yet.

Now don't you be worrying about Mack. I know you are--but don't. I got all the radio reports from Pearl Harbor and he is O.K. And furthermore he will stay O.K.

We are going to teach those Japs a lesson they will never forget! We have the finest Air Corps in the world and I am mighty proud to be in it!

It had to come sooner or later, and I am glad it has come now.

We moved into our new barracks a few days ago, and boy are they nice. Just like a big cement hotel!

Guess we will be here a long time, but sure wish I were in Pearl Harbor now. All the boys here are glad--and we are going to win!!

So don't you try to spoil my war by worrying!

After this is over, "Pinky" and I will come back on you and eat you out of house and home!

After all, this is my first war and some day I will be too old--gotta have my fling while I'm young.

I am sending up some presents and Xmas cards tomorrow. Hope you like them. They will be a little late though.

I sent Mack one by air mail today.

Write soon and remember--keep your chin up!

Love, Hoyt

P.S. Tell the kids I have sent them each a card. Merry Christmas to you all. You should be here in the Land of Tropical Sunshine. I went swimming at the beach Sunday--had a grand time.

I will write every week.

In the tropical sunshine, Hoyt kept a deep tan, and he enjoyed running races just as he did when on the track team at Martha Berry School for Boys. His family kept photos of him racing his fellow airmen--and being far ahead of them all.

Four days following the Pearl Harbor attack, he wrote as follows:

December 11, 1941

Dear Mom & All,

I received your letter yesterday and I was so sorry to hear how you all were worried. I know how you must feel about us being so far away, but please try to not worry much.

I am so proud to be part of the U.S. Air Corps now that I could almost burst! I feel like I am really doing something for my country now, and I know Mack must feel the same way.

We are on these islands to stop them before they can get to our homes, and we intend to do it--so don't you worry at all.

I guess it must be tough just sitting and waiting, but remember that Mothers & Dads have been doing it before. I can't make myself feel bad about it, because I think we are right, and I know we will win!

I sent a letter Monday by air. Did you get it? Mack will be O.K., because they will be waiting for the Japs there now.

Remember, don't worry at all!

Love, Hoyt

Hoyt was in Puerto Rico for 19 months, and was awarded a *Battle Star* for "gallantry in action" during the shelling of the base at San Juan. Then he was transferred to Langley Field in Virginia, and received his wings as an aerial engineer and instructor.

On April 22, 1943, he wrote as follows:

Dear Mom & All,

It's almost sun-up and I'm about ready to go to bed. Just brought in the last of the guards and now we have the next 24 hours off.

One of our planes went down abut 200 miles out to sea last night. Couldn't do much searching then, due to the fog, but all our planes are out now and we have hopes of finding them.

They had life rafts aboard, if they didn't go down too fast to use them. Most of the boys aboard are from my barracks.

Don't you think we're losing a lot of planes, because we're not, considering the number of missions we have to fly.

Sure was good to see Mack. I think he has changed some--especially his voice!

Now who said I talked differently?

He came out day before yesterday morning, and we stayed on the Field until I was relieved from guard duty, then we went to town.

I stayed over at his Hotel until he left about 10 yesterday morning.

Know you all were glad to see him--sure wish I could have gone back down with him and stayed a while. I may get another nine days off in June or July of this year.

Well, I'm sleepy as the devil, so I'm going to bed.

I guess you all are just about ready for work by now.

"Red" (Mack) said he wanted to plant some cotton when he got back.

Love, Hoyt

On May 3, 1943, Hoyt wrote to "Mom & All" about the death of a buddy.

His letter, in part, is as follows:

One of my best friends was killed today when he jumped from a plane that was in a spin! His chute failed to open. The pilot got control of the plane and landed it O.K.

Four of them bailed out and his was the only chute that failed to open. The other boys are swell fellows, but this one will really be missed here in our squadron.

We turned in his equipment this afternoon, and I moved into his room with the boys. We will have a military service for him tomorrow, and then the flights will go on.

Guess Mack is enjoying himself these days. Sure would like to be down with you.

Must go to bed now.

Love, Hoyt

A few weeks later, Hoyt wrote of a mishap with the plane he was on. Portions of his letter are as follows:

Started back flying Monday. Have lots of new crews to check out during the next two weeks. My bomber blew a tire and cracked up during the second take-off on Monday morning.

Banged the ole gal up pretty bad, but no one was hurt in the least.

Boy you really go for a ride when you blow a tire at 105 miles per hour! I got a man-size thrill out of it--but had to work the rest of that day and night getting the ship back to flying.

Had a recruit on board with me, and boy was he scared! It was his first flight.

Most of Hoyt's letters were addressed to "Mom & All," but on the first day of summer, 1943, he wrote only to his father. By then Perry Crump was doing well in the dairy business. Earlier, he had even gone to Athens, Georgia with an Agriculture Extension Agent, spent the night in a hotel for the first time, and talked on the radio about crop rotation and the benefits of red-tip clover in putting nitrogen back into depleted

farmlands. (Fields of red-tip clover can still be seen in Georgia.)

Hoyt's letter to his father is as follows:

June 21, 1943

Dear Daddy,

    I have wanted to write you for several days, but just haven't had the time until this morning.

    I'm off this morning because I was flying from six until ten o'clock last night. I was flying as aerial engineer for the Colonel and Major on a test flight for one of the new bombers.

    I was thinking about you then as I sat up in the glass nose by my instrument panel--bet you would have liked it if you could have been along--what about it?

    Or do you still think you had rather stay on the ground and raise good cows?

    I expect to get home for about a week in August, if possible. I'm looking forward to it--sure want to see all of you and the farm again.

    I'm taking care of my second payment this month. Thanks for sending my payment slip to me. Only drew a small part of my pay this month, so I'm darn near broke now, but I want to get Sis (Audrey) and Doyle something for a wedding present. What would you suggest?

    It will have to be some time after July 1st though--I won't have good pay until then.

    Seems funny Sis being married--only seems a very few years back that we chased her with worms. How old is she anyway? 18?

    Guess I'm darn near old enough to get married, huh? I wonder who and where is the gal for me.

    Think I'll wait until I go overseas again and bring back a wife that talks something you can't understand.

Love, Hoyt

(Hoyt had a girlfriend named Rosa during his time in Puerto Rico, and she had taught him to speak some Spanish.)

By summer of 1943, Hoyt's brother, Alton Crump, was ready to go into service. His parents wanted him to stay home and help on the farm, and Hoyt encouraged him to do that also. But Dessie and Perry Crump ended up with three sons to worry about in the midst of World War II--in spite of Hoyt's constant pleas for them not to. Hoyt's July 9, 1943 letter is as follows:

Friday noon--July 9

Dear Mom & All,

I received your last letter yesterday. I did get the cookies a few days ago, and enjoyed them very much.

Tell Wayne (youngest brother) I enjoyed his letter and am very proud of him, because it was real good writing and was worded nicely too.

We have this afternoon and tonight off and some of my crew and myself are going to the beach this afternoon.

We have been plenty busy here these past few weeks. Wednesday I flew eight and a half hours, with only thirty minutes on the ground for lunch. I was really fagged out that day. I had checked off three student aerial engineers for this month. Went up on a test flight Sat. night, and we stopped two of our engines (on the same side) and experimented with the ship for several hours.

Mom, the only way Alton can get in now is go to the board and tell them he wants Air Corps. If he gets in, I would advise him to take up Radio operation or Radar operation, that is if he wants to fly.

If he went into mechanics it would take quite a while to work up to aerial engineer and get his wings. It's true that mechanic schools now are not nearly as long as when I went through, but it still takes a long time to get up to Aerial Engineer and Crew Chief.

It took me quite a while, but now I have my own ship and its great, but really a responsibility having a quarter of a million dollar bomber and ten men working on it under you.
Hope he makes it O.K. whatever he takes up.
Tell him those wings feel good when they pin them on!

Love, Hoyt

In spite of Hoyt's glowing remarks about the Army Air Force, his brother Alton decided to join the Navy.

It was probably during Hoyt's furlough in August of 1943 that he came home to the farm and also made a trip back to the Martha Berry School to visit his former teachers. By that time, his classmates and other friends had graduated and gone out into the world, and a new crop of hopefuls was preparing for studies.

Wearing his Army Air Force uniform, Hoyt traveled to his old school the same way many other servicemen got from one place to another in those days.

He went to the nearest roadway and held out his thumb.

In the World War II era, no true American motorist dreamed of passing up a hitch-hiker wearing a uniform issued by Uncle Sam, so Hoyt had no long waits for transporation.

And on his way back to the Crump farm, he had more luck than he had anticipated.

When three young girls in a car saw him standing by the side of the road, they were more than willing to contribute to the cause of victory for the United States of America.

Hoyt Crump, the farm boy who could pick more cotton than anyone in Hart County, was tall and dark, and had a smile that could light up a cave at midnight. He had developed into what was being described by many as the most handsome man they had ever seen.

Therefore, when the girls gave him a lift, he gave them one in return.

Hoyt had a reputation as a "card counter," a fellow who could memorize all the cards that had been played in a game such as gin rummy. And therefore he usually won.

But on his journey from the Berry School to the farm on Route 3, Hartwell, he didn't need to memorize a thing--because he was dealt a perfect hand.

He no longer wondered who or where was the gal for him. She was sitting right beside him in the back seat of her cousin's car. She was a 17-year-old brunette beauty with a smile that matched his own. Her name was Margaret Ann Dobbs, and she was from Atlanta.

Hoyt and Margaret Ann began a long-distance romance by mail, but where his family was concerned, he kept his cards close to his chest and wore a poker face for a while.

The first hint he gave about Margaret Ann was included in a letter he wrote to Mom & All on November 6, 1943: *"A very pretty little girl from Atlanta sent me two hankies made from some parachute cloth I had sent her. A friend of mine bailed out from a burning plane with it."*

While at Langley Field, Hoyt was grounded and hospitalized in Woodrow Wilson Hospital in Staunton, Va. for several weeks with severe sinus problems, and he missed being in the air. He also wished he could have a chance to drop some bombs on the Nazis, and he wrote from the hospital: *"This is a heck of a way to fight a war--15 months in the States with nothing but sub patrols behind me."*

But in another letter while in the hospital, he wrote:

"Don't worry about me. Some of these boys here are pitiful. They have legs and arms shot off, and some have had their faces scarred something terrible."

On December 9, 1943, Hoyt wrote, in part: *"Hope you get electricity soon, because I know how much easier it will be for you then."* And he laid a portion of his cards on the table about Margaret Ann Dobbs for the first time, saying that he might bring her home to the farm during the Christmas season.

A few months later, on April 1, 1944, Margaret Ann became Mrs. Hoyt Woodrow Crump. The ceremony was held in Atlanta, and a reception took place at the Dobbs home on Lucille Avenue.

Sergeant and Mrs. Hoyt W. Crump at their wedding reception in the Atlanta home of the bride's parents.

The newlyweds lived in Savannah, Georgia for a time, after Hoyt was assigned to Chatham Field near there, where he served as a flight engineer and instructor.

And they moved into a garage apartment when he was transferred to MacDill Field in Tampa.

And it was on June 19, 1946 in Tampa that Margaret Ann promoted Sergeant Crump to the rank of father. The baby was a boy, and he was named Hoyt Woodrow Crump II.

Little Hoyt Woodrow Crump II held on tightly and dangled from his father's thumbs in this snapshot made in late summer of 1946. Hoyt II later said, "I had incredible upper body strength as a baby.

Sergeant Crump called his baby "the boy" and "Woody" in the letter he wrote to his family only six weeks before his death on Cold Mountain. It is as follows:

July 31, 1946

Dear Mom & All,

Margaret Ann and the boy are going to Atlanta by Eastern Airline Monday. They will stay about a week.

So maybe Mack or Alton one can come out sometime next week and get her and the boy and take them out to see you.

Her brother will not be home, so she won't have any way to get to Hartwell. Or if you all think it would be easier to just come out to see him that will be fine.

That's the only way I know for you to see him now, because I don't want him to be drug about on a bus as young as he is.

Any way you want to do, just write to M.A. at 1383 Lucille Avenue, S.W., Atlanta. Their phone is RA-6404 if you should need to call there.

I'm going to try hard to get an Army plane up the weekend of August 10-11 if I can. If I do I'll come out to see you all.

My outfit is going to settle down here, so guess we will all be up on a furlough now.

It just costs too much for both of us to come up from here, so I figured once a year would be enough for me, and I did want you to see "Woody" now.

So be sure and write to Atlanta as soon as you get this and tell her what you can do.

Love, Hoyt

As noted in his letters, Sergeant Crump's greatest regret during his time of service was that he did not get to go into an overseas combat zone. He was still yearning for more adventure while he was still young, but at the same time was a man who was happy in his role as husband and father, and one doing all he could for his country.

During the period following the end of World War II battles, he was trying to decide if he wanted to remain in the Army Air Force as a career, or enter civilian life when his tour was up.

His wife's cousin Ruth was married to Pete Clay, who was one of the managers of the Atlanta Airport, then known as Chandler Field. And Pete had been trying to persuade Hoyt to get out of service and work with him.

Earlier, Pete's son had been killed in a plane crash.

And as always, Sergeant Crump's thoughts were with the folks back home in Hart County, Georgia. In late August of 1946, he mailed his mother a special gift from him and Margaret Ann, something that Dessie might find useful.

The Crump home had electricity by then, and the gift was a little electric sewing machine that Margaret Ann had learned to sew on when she was a child.

Four days before the Cold Mountain tragedy, Hoyt wrote a postcard as follows:

Sept. 9, 1946

Dear Mom,

Yes, the little machine worked when I mailed it. Turn it upside down and you will see a screw on the bottom. Take it out and you can move the motor around until the belt is tight. When you put it back be sure the belt is tight and it will work.

Our boy is laughing lots now.

Love, Hoyt

Little Hoyt Woodrow "Woody" Crump II was only three-months-old when his father died on Cold Mountain. Sergeant Crump was age 27, a little more than two months away from his 28th birthday.

Margaret Ann Crump was 13 days from her 21st birthday when she became a widow.

Sergeant Crump's funeral was held on September 19, 1946 in Patterson Funeral Home Chapel in Atlanta.

During the service, Chaplain (Captain) Thomas A. Summey Jr. noted that Sergeant Crump was a flight engineer under Colonel Harding, who was succeeded by Major General Paul B. Wurtsmith in August of 1946. Sergeant Crump had been a flight engineer on several trips with General Wurtsmith prior to the fatal crash on Cold Mountain.

The Chaplain stated that Sergeant Crump held the *pre-Pearl Harbor Ribbon with Star; Good Conduct Medal, and the American Theatre Ribbon with two Battle Stars.*

Dessie Crump requested a copy of the Chaplain's remarks after the funeral. As it had been with the funerals of the other four men who died in the bomber crash, her son's casket remained closed.

Sergeant Crump's remains were buried in Plot 34 in the "Garden of Memories" section of Atlanta's West View Cemetery, one of the largest and oldest cemeteries in the country. It was said to be a place where "anybody who *was* anybody" was laid to rest.

*****

HIS BOY'S JOURNEY

Sergeant Crump's young widow was as smart and level-headed as she was pretty. After the bomber crash on Cold Mountain, she and her infant son moved back to Atlanta to be near her family, and they lived with her parents for a few years.

Margaret Ann had one brother Roy Dobbs Jr., who was a star on the track team at Georgia Tech. He had admired his young brother-in-law greatly, and remembered Sergeant Crump as being "the strongest man" he had ever met, in spite of the fact that he was almost thin as a rail.

After a time, Margaret Ann used the insurance money she received following her husband's death to obtain a lot and build a house in walking distance of Georgia Military Academy in Atlanta (now Woodward Military Academy).

The lot was actually part of the Academy, and officials agreed to let a house be built there only because Sergeant Crump had expressed a hope that his son could receive an education at a Military School when he was older. There was also an agreement that the lot would revert back to the Academy if it was not used for the Crump residence in the future.

In 1950, when Hoyt II was age four-and-a-half, Margaret Ann Crump married again. And just as Marie Okerbloom had married a man who was the opposite of her Pete, Margaret Ann's second husband was the opposite of her Hoyt.

Jeff Askew Jr., an order clerk at Fulton Supply Company in Atlanta, was two years older than Margaret Ann. He was a good man, and nice-looking, but was not the athletic "ladies' man" type nor the adventure-seeking type that Sergeant Hoyt Crump had been.

But he and Sergeant Crump had a lot in common nevertheless, because both had grown up poor.

Askew's father had an alcohol problem, and his mother died in a car wreck when he was six-years-old.

Being the oldest in the family, he had to take on the role of mother to his younger siblings, and was trying to earn money to help support the family when he was only eight-years-old, by activities such as selling magazines.

Margaret Ann's second husband was also unlike Sergeant Crump in that he was about the most unlikely soldier anyone could imagine.

Yet, at the height of World War II, Technical Sergeant Jeff Askew found himself in a unit of General George Patton's Third Army, which went ashore in France three days after D-Day, June 6, 1944.

Sergeant Askew was the company clerk, and did not go to the front lines in battle. But part of his job as clerk was almost worse, at least where he was concerned.

Because they had such different personalities and interests, Hoyt Crump II didn't have a very close relationship with his stepfather during his growing-up years. And Jeff Askew never brought up the subject of World War II.

However, when Hoyt II was a grown man, he went home for a visit, and one evening he sat on the steps with his stepfather, who shared his memories of the war for the first time.

The story unfolded as golden colors of sunset spread above the western horizon. It was not an easy topic for Mr. Askew, and he broke down several times during the telling.

He said that his unit raced to reinforce the embattled 101st Airborne at the Battle of the Bulge, and rockets and artillery fire screamed over his head and exploded nearby on numerous occasions.

As company clerk, it was his duty to identify bodies of his buddies that had been killed in battle, collect their dog-tags and personal belongings, make a report, and arrange for burial of their bodies.

He said he would identify four or five bodies, then go off to the side, cry, and vomit. Then he'd go back and identify four or five more, and go cry and throw up again. He kept up that pattern until his terrible task was completed.

The man who became stepfather to Sergeant Hoyt Crump's son might not have volunteered to recover bodies on Cold Mountain in 1946, but certainly would have fulfilled that duty if called upon to do so.

Hoyt Crump II will always be thankful that Jeff Askew was finally able to share his World War II experiences with him. It allowed him to see him in a totally new light, and forged a bond that had been missing in earlier times.

Hoyt II said of his stepfather, "I think his service in World War II showed extraordinary bravery and heroism in its own right."

*****

MARGARET ANN'S CAREER

After Sergeant Crump's death, his son was no longer called "Woody," but was known as "Little Hoyt" until he was 13-years-old.

His stepfather provided well for the family, and his mother had an illustrious career of her own.

By age six, little Margaret Ann was making doll clothes on a toy sewing machine, and by age nine had graduated to a small electric Singer model. (The one that was sent to Sergeant Crump's mother in 1946.)

Margaret Ann graduated from Commercial High School in Atlanta, at that time a school for potential artists and business people. And after her widowhood, she earned a reputation as one of the finest seamstresses in the city.

She specialized in creating bridal gowns--and also designing and making clothing and costumes for movies and television. Some of the shows using her outfits were the family comedy *My Little Margie*, starring Gail Storm; and westerns *U.S. Marshall* and *Sheriff of Cochise*, both starring John Bromfield.

The family was well-acquainted with actor/comedian Jim Backus, whose extensive career included the role of Thurston Howell III on TV's *Gilligan's Island*, and the voice of cartoon character *Mr. McGoo*.

Hoyt II recalled that other "Hollywood types" were in and out of his house throughout his young years.

At age eight, Hoyt II welcomed a half-sister, Peggy Ann Askew, into the family. She became a Licensed Practical Nurse (LPN) and worked in nursing homes and in private practice. By 2005, she and her husband, Mickey Smith, resided in Jackson, Georgia.

Two years before his sister's birth, Hoyt II enrolled in the first grade at Georgia Military Academy, and it was there that he received 12 years of education, as his father had wished.

He excelled in the school, and developed a strong patriotism that never faltered through the years--but his service to his fellowmen would be in an area other than the Armed Forces.

HOYT W. CRUMP II, MD

Under a scholarship provided by the federal government, because his father died on Cold Mountain during the World War II period and he was his only surviving son, Hoyt II was able to complete studies at Emory University in Atlanta.

And his scholarship continued through part of his four years at the Medical College of Georgia.

Dr. Hoyt W. Crump II became a family practitioner with a clinic in Royston, Georgia, not far from the place where his father became the best cotton picker in Hart County.

In thinking about the tragedy that claimed the life of the father he never knew, Dr. Crump said, "Everything happens for a reason."

Like that of countless others, Dr. Crump's belief is that the reason for a terrible event can't be seen or understood right away, but it is all in God's plan and will unfold in His time.

Because his father's death led to an education he likely would not have had otherwise, by 2005 Dr. Crump had been able to assist young mothers in bringing over 600 new lives into the world

He had been at special events where someone would have died without his quick action, and he had brought health and healing to young and old, and comfort in his patients' final hours.

"And I've witnessed many results of modern medical science that might fall in the category of miracle," he said.

Since he was his mother's only son, he was in a draft category that kept him out of the Vietnam War. He said he had mixed feelings about that war, and about not being part of it. One of his best friends, Captain Bobby Jones, was the only flight surgeon killed in Vietnam, and another friend from medical school, Captain Terry Ward, M.D., had many narrow escapes.

*****

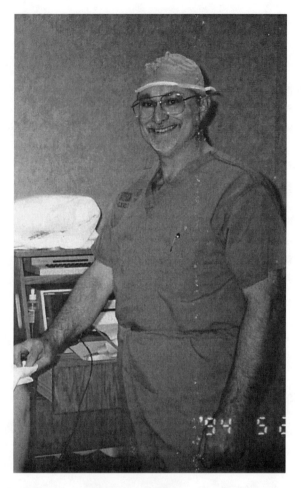

Dr. Hoyt W. Crump II had delivered over 600 babies by 2005, and had witnessed results of medical science "that might fall in the category of miracle."

For his work, Dr. Crump received many honors through the years. And in 1979, he was among physicians named Fellows of the American Academy of Family Physicians, based on continuing studies and a certifying examination.

The ceremony, in which honorees wore caps and gowns, was held in the city in which Dr. Crump's parents were married and where Sergeant Hoyt W. Crump's remains were buried.

The son of the poor farm boy who had to drop out of school after eighth grade and didn't receive a high school diploma until age 21, became a Fellow of the American Academy of Family Physicians before a crowd of 2,500 in the Atlanta Civic Center.

*****

A LESSON ON THE CRUMP FARM

As years went by, Dr. Crump remained close to his father's family, and he cherishes the memory of a time when he was a freshman at Emory University and spent several days of his spring break on the Crump farm.

Athletic like Sergeant Crump, he worked out with the Emory wrestling team and was involved in every sport offered at the school. And he felt he was in as good a shape as anyone his age could possibly be.

His grandfather, Perry Crump, was in his 70s then, and Hoyt's plan was to pitch in and be a priceless help to the old fellow.

Little did the young man suspect he was about to receive a lesson that was not included in any of his college textbooks.

After getting up at 4 a.m. to milk cows and spending the rest of the day on various other farm chores, the Crumps' muscular grandson had never been as tired in his entire life. "My grandfather out-worked me two to one," he recalled.

He said he was so exhausted after that first day that he fell asleep in a chair in his grandparents' living room long before bedtime.

When he woke up, his grandfather was still watching TV, with no sign of fatigue.

During those few days of spring, the college boy gained a deep and abiding respect and admiration for the erstwhile sharecropper, and others like him, who had gotten their hands dirty, poured sweat, and helped mold America into a great nation.

*****

Perry Crump died at age 84 on February 7, 1979 after a lengthy illness.

By then, death had already claimed three of his and Dessie's five sons--Hoyt, Mack, and Jack.

In 1954, Mack Crump died in a freak accident involving an electric fence. It was less than eight years after Hoyt's death on Cold Mountain, and was also on a Friday the 13th.

And in 1975, his brother Jack also died on the 13th day of the month, but not on a Friday.

By 1979, the little brother Sergeant Hoyt Crump had praised for his writing was Staff Sergeant Wayne Crump, a National Guard Recruiter in his home territory.

All five of Perry and Dessie's sons had served in the Armed Forces--Hoyt in the Army Air Force, Mack and Alton in the Navy; and Jack and Wayne in the Army.

Perry's funeral was held in Strickland Funeral Home Chapel in Hartwell, and burial was in Nancy Hart Memorial Park.

The family requested that flowers be omitted and memorials for Perry be made instead to the building fund of Cedar Creek Baptist Church.

The couple had been married 61 years.

*****

Like the mother of General Paul B. Wurtsmith, the mother of Sergeant Hoyt W. Crump lived to age 91.

Dessie Ayers Crump died on November 18, 1992, 10 days before what would have been Sergeant Crump's 74th birthday, had he lived as he expected when he wrote during World War II, *"...some day I will be too old--gotta have my fling while I'm young."*

Dessie's survivors included sons Alton and Wayne Crump, daughters Audrey McCall and Jan Burgess; 10 grandchildren, and 19 great-grandchildren. (By 2005, only Alton and Jan were still living, and the Crump farm was no longer in the family.)

Following her funeral in Cedar Creek Baptist Church, Dessie's body was buried beside Perry's in Nancy Hart Memorial Park.

Dr. Crump was a pallbearer at both his grandparents' funerals.

*****

THE DOCTOR'S FAMILY

In 1975, Dr. Crump was working in the emergency room of Shallowford Community Hospital in the Dunwoody section of Atlanta when he was invited to a party for the hospital staff.

He was "into horses" then, and during the party was showing photos of those he owned to a friend.

A pretty Registered Nurse, Laura Lee Righton, walked up and asked to have a look. She liked horses too.

A native of Stone Mountain, Georgia, Lee Righton worked in the hospital's Intensive Care Unit, and had not met Dr. Crump prior to the party.

Like Richard Oakley and Joyce Kali, it was love at first sight, and the couple married two and a half months later. Skipping the usual ceremonial fanfare and finery, they eloped and kept it sweet and simple.

Until Lee Crump's semi-retirement in 1982, she helped Dr. Crump with cardiac patient evaluation and counseling for new mothers in the La Leche League, which promotes breast-feeding of infants.

Beloved by his patients, Dr. Crump's list includes some who drive 90 miles each year for their annual checkup.

The skills and caring of Dr. and Mrs. Crump were among those lauded in the May 25, 1980 edition of *The Advocate*, a Christian magazine. Titled *Angels at Work*, the article was written by Rev. Charles E. Bradshaw.

The two sons and daughter of Dr. and Mrs. Hoyt Crump II and grandchildren of Sergeant Hoyt W. Crump are: Roy Van Keuren Crump, who by 2005 was involved in computer science, as an original art and graphic artist in Silicon Valley, California; Charles Hoyt Crump, who was employed in a NASCAR memorabilia store in Gainesville, Georgia and also had a business creating web sites for small companies; and Dessie Lee Crump Mazhar, whose husband works with computers at Warner Robbins Air Force Base near Macon, Georgia. There were two grandchildren, Noah Hoyt Crump and Alyssa Lee Mazhar, great-grandchildren of Sergeant Crump.

This 1992 portrait shows Dr. Hoyt W. Crump II and wife, Lee, and their sons and daughter (grandchildren of Sergeant Hoyt W. Crump), left to right: Charles Hoyt Crump, Dessie Lee Crump, and Roy Van Keuren Crump.

In 2005, Dr. and Mrs. Crump resided in Franklin Springs, Georgia, not far from his clinic in Royston.

They were members of Hartwell First Presbyterian Church, and they also had many friends of the Pentacostal Holiness faith, which had headquarters in Franklin Springs.

In missions sponsored by the Presbyterian Church, Dr. Crump and his wife and son, Roy, traveled to Mexico at various times and helped build houses for the poor.

"The projects were similiar to Habitat for Humanity," Dr. Crump explained.

For many years, Dr. and Mrs. Crump enjoyed trail riding in their leisure time, and kept quite a few horses for that purpose, and for showing, but Mrs. Crump's eventual need for knee surgery led them into other pasttimes--and by 2005 their favorite was attending NASCAR races with friends.

After a race at Bristol, Tennessee in August of 2004, they drove to the Cold Mountain area, but did no hiking.

It was in the autumn of 1973 that Dr. Crump and his uncles, Jack and Wayne Crump, hiked up Cold Mountain, but were unable to find the spot where their father and brother died 27 years earlier, at age 27.

A short time later, when the leaves were off the trees, Jack Crump went back with two of his friends, and that time they did locate the crash site and brought home several souvenirs from the bomber.

*****

Before the bomber hit Cold Mountain on that near-autumn day in 1946, Staff Sergeant Hoyt W. Crump did not have a chance to pen one last note to his family, pleading once again, *"DON'T WORRY ABOUT ME!"*

He didn't have a chance to glimpse the future of his young widow and infant son.

If such had been possible, and if Sergeant Crump could have added one more line to his final message, he might have written the same words his son spoke as a physician.

The Sergeant's farewell note might have ended with *"EVERYTHING HAPPENS FOR A REASON."*

Part Three:

BACK TO COLD MOUNTAIN
and
THE REST OF THE STORY

NO REST FOR THE MAJOR

Several days after the recovery process on Cold Mountain, 11-year-old Mack Warren of Lake Logan Road and a few older boys were on their way to the crash site when they met several military men coming down.

Mack was too young to recognize ranks from insignias on uniforms, so he had no way of knowing if one of the men was Major Theodore J. Hieatt. The boys only knew that some were officers, and one was not pleased with the way something had been done during the last day of the recovery.

As the boys passed by the men, who had paused momentarily, Mack heard one ask who had been in charge of a last detail on The Mountain. Another replied that it was "Sergeant ....," and the officer who asked the question responded with another question, "You mean *Private*, don't you?"

And Mack wasn't too young to figure that some Sergeant was going to get busted as soon as the men got back to the base in Greenville.

After the recovery had been completed to everyone's satisfaction, the War Department issued orders to abandon the wreckage. A yellow cross was painted on one of the plane's wings to mark it as an "old wreck" and keep future air and ground searchers from mistaking it for a new crash or an old one that had not yet been located.

Plane crashes dating back to 1943 kept Major Hieatt and his ground search crews busy following their difficult duties on The Mountain, and the process again boldly illustrated the fact that the mountain wilderness areas of North Carolina and Tennessee did not readily give up their secrets.

In late October of 1946, Major Hieatt resumed the ground search for the UC-78 Cessna which took off from Charlotte, North Carolina enroute to Nashville, Tennessee on January 31, 1944 with three Army officers and an atomic scientist on board.

Called a "Bamboo Bomber," or "Bobcat," the UC-78 was a medium-sized aircraft designed as a trainer for bombing missions. It had twin-blade propellers, two 245 horsepower engines, a large cabin, and was covered in olive-drab fabric. It could travel 750 miles without refueling.

The best clues from those who witnessed the plane in flight indicated that it had gone down somewhere in the mountains, but extensive ground and air searches by the military, Civil Air Patrol, and search-and-rescue teams with the Park Services of Pisgah National Forest and the Great Smoky Mountains National Park had found no sign of the wreckage after almost two years.

On September 10, 1946, three days before the B-25 bomber crash on Cold Mountain, loggers in the Maggie Valley area of Haywood County reported finding some olive-drab material, like that on the UC-78, and so Major Hieatt and his crews again focused in that area after the Cold Mountain recovery.

By late December of 1946, the Major was suspecting the piece that had been found was from a small plane that crashed in 1943, not from the UC-78. The pilots involved in the 1943 crash had survived, and the Major was trying to contact them and gain information that might be helpful.

Apparently he did not gain support right away in his belief that the olive-drab material was not from the UC-78, but Major Hieatt and his men did receive a little break in their search, because harsh winter bore down and covered mountain boulders with ice, thus making climbing impossible. So the ground search had to be called off for about two weeks.

By mid-January of the new year, 1947, rains had melted the ice, and Major Hieatt and a ground party of 18 servicemen from Greenville Air Base set up headquarters in the LeFaine Hotel on Main Street in Waynesville and continued the search for the missing Cessna in the mountains around Maggie Valley.

In addition to the ground search personnel, the Army sent in five vehicles and a gasoline tanker to fuel two Army search planes.

After residents of Maggie Valley were interviewed, an Army detachment set up camp at Cataloochee Ranch, where some residents of the area had seen or heard a plane pass overhead during a heavy snowstorm in 1944.

An object resembling part of a plane was reported seen in Paul's Gap, and the search party headed to that area, with three servicemen becoming temporarily lost in the process.

In early February, 1947 two Air Rescue Helicopters were sent in to join in the search. A helicopter had not landed in Haywood County prior to that time, and the two "whirlybirds" created a lot of excitement. One was from Selfridge Air Base at Detroit, the final departure point for the B-25 bomber that crashed on Cold Mountain less than five months earlier.

After finding nothing in Haywood County, Major Hieatt set up headquarters at the Asheville-Hendersonville Airport, and more helicopters, trucks, and equipment were brought in.

By then, the Major had been combing the North Carolina mountains for half a year, and his search for the missing UC-78 Cessna was finally called off after it was decided that the olive-drab material that launched the renewed search was indeed from the plane that crashed in 1943.

(And by 2005, in spite of the most diligent searches by many different search-and-recovery units, the UC-78 Cessna, Army officers, and atomic scientist were still officially listed as missing. The mountains had revealed nothing, and the mystery remained.)

In October of 1947, Major Hieatt conducted an air search for a DC-3 cargo plane which had taken off in Massachusetts, picked up a load of 25,000 baby chickens in Charlotte, and was headed to Gainesville, Georgia. There were three men on board.

The air search was futile, but the plane wreckage was discovered a short time later by bear-hunters, including Jack Frady and "Beanie" Moody, who were among those at the scene of the B-25 bomber crash on Cold Mountain shortly after the recovery process.

The men were hunting in the Caney Fork Section of Jackson County, N.C., when they noticed a dreadful odor and followed it to the source. Neither the three men nor the baby chicks had survived.

In 1948, Major Theodore J. Hieatt was sent to Japan, and he retired with the rank of Lieutenant Colonel in 1953.

He was active in the Air Force Reserves until 1959.

And it was during the late 1950s that his vast experience in the field of intelligence earned him a civilian job as Deputy Chief of the Air Force Intelligence Office at Wright-Patterson Air Force Base in Ohio. He became involved in the Air Force's *Project Blue Book*, which had begun in 1951 and listed thousands of reports of UFO (Unidentified Flying Object) sightings.

The *Blue Book*, which had only a small percentage of sightings in the "unexplained" category, raised the ire of UFO researchers and enthusiasts like noted author Donald Keyhoe, and the many citizens who swore they had seen something other than natural objects such as meteorites or the planet Venus, or man-made devices such as weather balloons.

Theodore J. Hieatt served as the "public relations expert" on a distinguished panel looking into the UFO phenomenon.

The panel chairman was the renowned astronomy and physics professor, Dr. J. Allen Hynek, who entered the project as a skeptic but came to believe that some UFOs could be spaceships controlled by intelligent beings from other planets.

UFO sightings were rampant worldwide in the early 1950s, but not all were reported. One such sighting occurred near Cold Mountain less than five years after the B-25 bomber crash.

In 2005, Thomas Lynn Wells of Arden, N.C., a retired college instructor who brought home souvenirs from the bomber wreckage when he was in the sixth grade, said he remembered the UFO incident "as clear as if it had happened yesterday."

It was in the spring of 1952, when he was a junior at Bethel High School, that he saw something hovering in the sky between his home on Love Joy Road and Hen Top mountain.

He called for his father, Tom Wells, to come quick.

Caught in the rays of late afternoon sun, the object was huge and cigar-shaped, and was emitting no sound. And it was low enough for the father and son to see markings on its side.

They emphasized that they were just "markings"--not any kind of numbers or letters they had seen before, in any language.

As the two observers stood spellbound for several minutes, the object assumed a vertical position and went straight up and out of sight--still making no sound at all.

The Wellses did not make an official report about their unusual experience, and told only friends and neighbors--who knew them well, knew that they were telling the truth, and were not mistaking some ordinary aircraft or anything else for what they had seen.

The sighting by Thomas Lynn Wells and his father was not the only one in Haywood County and other parts of western North Carolina in 1952, and there were numerous UFO reports from the area of the atomic facility at Oak Ridge, Tennessee.

*****

LOST GIRLS

Around four years prior to the Wells' sighting of the UFO, some sixth grade girls had an unforgettable venture on Cold Mountain.

It was on a beautiful early spring day in 1948 when the girls, all members of a Sunday School class at East Fork Baptist Church, decided they wanted to go to the bomber crash site following the morning worship service.

After changing into blue jeans and light jackets, they set off on their journey.

Loy Henson Jr., whose nickname was "June Bug," agreed to serve as the girls' guide. The hike began at Crawford Creek, and soon The Mountain was alive with shrieks and giggles galore.

June Bug was 15-years-old then. His younger sister, Clara, was a member of the Sunday School class, but didn't go on the hike that day.

As the familiar trappings of civilization were left behind, June Bug added more drama to the outing by telling his sister's 11-and 12-year-old friends some scary mountain stories.

After they viewed the bomber wreckage and headed back down The Mountain, Joanna Neal and Joyce Webb and one of their friends veered off from the main group in search of a clump of big bushes or trees that could serve as "nature's restroom door."

And when they later tried to catch up with the others, they couldn't find the trail they had left, and couldn't see or hear any of the group further down The Mountain.

When the main group reached a certain point in the descent, one of the girls noticed that some were missing, and June Bug headed back up The Mountain in search of them. But after yelling their names and looking all over, he found no clue to their whereabouts.

Meanwhile, on another part of Cold Mountain, the three lost girls came to a fork in a trail they had discovered, and they had no idea which one to take. "I think we'd better pray," Joanna said.

And they began following a creek.

By then, the weather, which had earlier seemed like perfect mountain springtime, took a drastic turn, as it was prone to do on Cold Mountain.

It became bitterly cold and wind began hurling bluish snow.

June Bug's scary tales had been meant for fun, but now Joanna, Joyce, and their friend were genuinely frightened.

After they wandered on The Mountain for what seemed like ages, a wondrous sight came into view. It was gray smoke curling from the chimney of a small cabin.

The girls had no idea who lived there, or what might happen if they approached, but they knew they had to get to that little house as soon as possible.

"It was the neatest cabin we'd ever seen," Joanna recalled.

A woman was inside, and her baby was sitting on the floor. A fire was roaring in a large fireplace.

In the eyes of the girls, the woman was an angel sent from a place a whole lot higher than Cold Mountain.

Her name was Nettie Gibson, and she told the shivering youngsters, "You all get in here and get warm! You look like you're froze to death!"

Nettie explained that her husband, Earl Gibson, a logger, was away delivering a load of timber. "If he was here, he could carry you right on down to Dix Creek," she said.

But since he wouldn't be returning any time soon, Nettie told the girls exactly how to get safely down The Mountain. And after they had thawed out in front of the heavenly fire, they thanked their special angel and headed on their way.

Meanwhile, word about the missing girls had spread in the communities below Cold Mountain, and search parties were formed at Crawford Creek, Lenoir Creek, and Dix Creek.

When June Bug finally had to give up and come down from The Mountain, his feet were so cold that his mother feared they were frostbitten.

It was nearing dusk when those gathered at Dix Creek saw the lost girls approaching in the distance.

Joanna's mother was among those at that site.

"I thought she'd come running and give me a big hug," Joanna recalled. But instead, Mrs. Neal gave her daughter a sound whipping, because she had risked her life by leaving the main group, and had almost worried the life out of her family and many other folks as well.

"She wore me out!," Joanna said with a laugh provided by intervening years.

By 2005, Joanna was the widow of Steve Penland, and Joyce Webb was the widow of Grady Birchfield.

Joanna noted that, through the years, she offered their 1948 episode as a cautionary tale for her children and grandchildren, and for anyone planning to hike up Cold Mountain for the first time.

*****

MACK'S MOUNTAINS TO CLIMB

Mack Ledbetter, the Bethel High School student who was at the scene shortly after the bomber crash and helped with the recovery process, was faced with more difficult mountains to climb in years to come.

The next to youngest of the six children (five sons and one daughter) of Allie and J.P. Ledbetter, he grew up on Love Joy Road near Chambers Cove and a short distance from Riverside Baptist Church on Lake Logan Road. And before finishing his education at Bethel High School, he and a friend, Billy Erwin, went to Baltimore, Maryland, where they were employed by the Glenn L. Martin Aircraft Corporation.

Billy returned home after a short time, but Mack continued to work in the plant's wing assembly department until 1951, when he was drafted into the Army at age 19.

He served in the Third Infantry Division during the Korean War. And while being flown back to the combat zone following a few days of R & R (Rest and Recreation) in Japan, his plane developed a problem and passengers were told to strap on parachutes.

What Mack remembered most about the incident was that his thoughts flashed back to Cold Mountain when he looked at his parachute's ripcord--and recognized it as being the same as one of the souvenirs he had retrieved from scene of the B-25 bomber crash.

Fortunately, there was no need for Mack to use his parachute, and the plane continued on to a safe landing.

After a blind date arranged during a furlough by one of his Army buddies, Mack and Ethel Watts began corresponding by mail and seeing each other as often as possible. A native of Franklin, N.C., Ethel was working at Wellco Shoe Factory in Hazelwood (Haywood County) when the two met.

They were married in 1953, the same year Mack was discharged from the Army. (He remained in the Army Reserves for two more years.)

In time, the couple became parents of three daughters and a son.

Mack worked for a short while in The Company Store for employees of Champion Paper and Fiber Company in Canton, then spent 40 years with the American Enka Corporation, producers of industrial rayon and nylon. The plant was in Buncombe County, adjoining Haywood.

In 1994, Mack retired, and might have looked forward to spending a lot of time in outdoor activities. But because his 10 years prior to retirement were spent in a job that required little physical exertion, he was in no condition to do the hunting and mountain hiking he had enjoyed in his younger years.

And in 1995 he suffered a stroke that robbed him of much of the use of both legs.

From the front porch of the couple's home near Silver Bluff nursing facility in the Bethel community, there is a clear view of Cold Mountain, and its signature Swag seemed to beckon to the man who not only couldn't climb, but had to learn to walk, just as he had done as a small child.

"God, please help me walk again," Mack prayed.

He might have prayed to be able to climb Cold Mountain once more, but under the circumstances that seemed to be far too much to request.

But Mack's prayers were answered, and then some. He not only walked again--he hiked back to the B-25 crash site he had first seen as a teenager.

At age 73 in 2004, Mack estimated that he had made at least 75 trips up Cold Mountain, and many of those were completed after he recovered from his stroke.

Some of the people Mack accompanied to the bomber crash site at various times were: his daughters, Verda Davis and Lorna Ledbetter; his grandson, Nate Riggeal, (son of his daughter Deborah Riggeal); his son, Doyle Ledbetter; his nephew, Richard Clark; Shelby Hopkins, Wayne Suggs, Clyde Reece, David Moore, Barbara Bolden, Gay Calhoun, Carolyn Janey, Ray Reece, Corley Chambers, Danny Sorrells, J.P. Mashburn, Mitzi and Dan Warren, and Donald and Caroline Taylor, all of Haywood County; and Kathy Odbody of Lincoln, Nebraska.

Mack recalled that in 1946 Corley Chambers, then age 63, said to him, "Mack, I'm going to 'kick the bucket' before long, and I'd like to make just one more trip up Cold Mountain. Will you go with me?"

Corley's wish was granted, and because he was not able to hike, he and Mack made the trek on horseback.

As he had predicted, Corley died not long after he made his final visit to The Mountain.

Mack's brothers Roy and Jay Ledbetter have also accompanied him up Cold Mountain many times. (Jay was at the scene of the bomber crash on Sunday, September 15, 1946 when the recovery team continued its task, and he helped with the process.)

Nearly half a century after Mack's Army years were finished, he and Ethel were honored with visits by three of his Korean War buddies and their wives: Joel and Bonnie Whitehead of Fairhope, Alabama; John and Nancy Watson of Ediston, Mississippi; and Hubert and Betty Legg of Blairsville, Georgia.

Nothing would have pleased Mack more than to have led them to the top of Cold Mountain. However, his friends were not able to tackle such a strenuous outing, and so they admired The Mountain's eternal beauty, and pondered its sad 1946 history, from the comfort of the Ledbetters' porch.

In 1996, Mack volunteered to trim the hiking trails in the Middle Prong Section near Sunburst, above Lake Logan, and later he added trails in the Shining Rock Wilderness, which includes Cold Mountain.

As a boy at the site of the bomber crash, he never dreamed he would return again and again, and do so as a man older than the parents of the men who died at that spot.

Mack agreed that there are many miracles that happen in many lives every day, if they can only be recognized for what they are.

Regardless of what the coming years would hold in store, Cold Mountain would always be an important part of Mack's own miracle at a crucial time in his life.

Mack Ledbetter and an old railroad relic found during one of his many hikes on and around Cold Mountain.

*****

Lessley D. Griffin of Cruso, author of *Cold Mountain Hunter*, published in 2004, was born 16 years after the bomber crash.

His father, Roy Griffin, and other seasoned hunters, helped make Cold Mountain a place he will cherish for a lifetime. In his book, he wrote of the "mysterious and unexplainable" feeling that he experienced when walking on what hunters named "Plane Crash Trail."

While hunting with his father at age 10, Lessley found a piece of riveted aluminum from the bomber, and carried part of it in his hunting vest since that time.

"I'm not sure I'm a believer in luck," he wrote, *"but for some reason I feel a lot more comfortable knowing it's in my pocket."*

Austin Thompson of Cruso, a college student in 2005, also kept a small piece of the bomber he found on The Mountain.

Austin's grandfather, Army Sergeant Max Thompson, grew up on Old Mine Road in the Dix Creek section near Cruso, and spent most of his life in that area.

For extraordinary heroism in World War II, Sergeant Thompson was awarded *The Congressional Medal of Honor*, the highest tribute that can be paid a member of the Armed Forces. (Only 464 WW II servicemen were recipients of the Medal.)

Sergeant Thompson died at age 74 in 1996.

Austin cherishes his grandfather's Medal of Honor--and also the piece of the B-25 bomber.

Both are tangible symbols of the courage and sacrifice required to keep America strong and free.

*****

Austin Thompson of Cruso holds the Congressional Medal of Honor which was presented to his grandfather, Army Sergeant Max Thompson, for heroism in World War II. Another of his cherished possessions is a piece of the B-25 bomber found on Cold Mountain.

*****

THE ROY MOODY STORY

It is doubtful that anyone who was not a relative or friend of those who died in the B-25 crash on Cold Mountain was more affected by the event than Roy Chambers Moody of Waynesville.

Roy was 67-years-old (2005) when he said, *"If I had been an atheist, what happened in my life because of the bomber crash would certainly have made a believer out of me."*

His avid interest in the 1946 disaster set up a chain of events that expanded his horizons in many ways--and may have saved his life!

It was a long and winding mountain road that Roy traveled to becoming known as *Haywood County's Bomber Crash Historian.* And the hardest thing for him to understand was why the memory of the crash completely vanished from his mind for decades.

A very unscientific, yet perhaps reasonable answer, was that the memory was just lying in wait, gathering steam, and preparing to explode--*when the time was right.*

*****

THE BOY WHO WAS LEFT OUT

In Roy Moody's childhood days, children had few toys, especially after the start of World War II, when rationing went into effect. Roy was fascinated with anything that had wheels--wagons, cars, trucks, buses, and airplanes.

And it was a passion that he never outgrew.

As a child, he made his own toy vehicles out of such things as thread spools, corncobs, match sticks, rubber bands, crayons, and folded paper.

Some cereal boxes during that era had "cut-outs" of World War II aircraft, and cards inside with photos and descriptions of planes, and Roy saved them all. And as he played with his handmade toys and cut-outs, he dreamed of traveling far beyond Lake Logan, the Pigeon River, and the lofty rise of Cold Mountain.

Because of poor eyesight, Roy's father, Ned Moody, was unable to drive a vehicle, therefore the family did not own a car. But little Roy was happy to be able to ride often with his Uncle Bob James in his 1940 Ford coupe, and with his cousin, Floyd Burnette, who drove his Aunt Alma Chambers' 1937 Ford.

In those days, Floyd was young and prone to some flamboyant driving, and riding with him was often scary, but Roy loved every second of it. And when his cousin came home as First Lieutenant Floyd W. Burnette, an Army Air Force pilot, the thrill of being able to ride in a car with him was beyond measure. (Before the end of World War II, Lieutenant Burnette had flown 51 bombing missions over Germany in a B-24 Liberator.)

Other exciting times for Roy and his pals were the days when state workers arrived with their big equipment and scraped the gravel roads in the Lake Logan and Bethel areas. "Bill Wells drove the road grader by our house," Roy recalled, "and Vess Owen also operated one." He said children looked up to them "like kids look up to NASCAR drivers today."

Having been thus inspired by his auto-driving kin and the men who operated the road maintenance machines, little Roy stood at the rail by the rock wall at Riverside Baptist Church, looked down the two-lane gravel road leading to the town of Canton, and daydreamed: "Someday, I'll drive a car down that road."

It was a dream that intensified when his Uncle Bob James gave him one of the old rubber Goodyear tires from his 1940 Ford coupe--a priceless gift indeed.

Roy was five-years-old then, and before long tires were becoming scarce because the war effort was in full swing.

When Roy wasn't playing with his tire, it was stored under the "porch basement" at the nearby home of his grandparents, Charlie W. and Sallie Osborne Moody.

The space under their porch was a deep open area where men graded tobacco in late autumn and Sallie Moody stored her canned goods.

And it was a time when no one locked their doors at night.

One day, a couple of young men stopped Roy while he was rolling his tire, and asked, "How much will you take for that?" And Roy quickly replied that his tire was not for sale.

He wouldn't have parted with it for anything.

But several days later, he went to get his treasure from under his grandparents' porch--and discovered that it had been stolen.

"I cried for three days," he recalled.

*****

Roy remembered that on Friday, September 13, 1946, it rained all day, and there was no chance for students at Cecil Elementary School to play outside. He was nine-years-old then, and in the fourth grade. His teacher was Pearl Hargrove, and his Aunt Alma Chambers taught first grade at the school.

The rain continued all night, and was not completely over by Saturday morning. Nevertheless, Saturday was a special day for Roy, because he and his mother, Nell, were going to town. "Mother made a shopping trip to Canton every two or three weeks," Roy said.

And on that Saturday, September 14, they stood in a slow drizzle waiting for the "work bus," which carried employees of the Champion Paper and Fiber Company in Canton to and from three shifts. People who didn't work in the mill could ride the bus for a 10-cent fare.

During their wait, they saw a small plane flying slowly through the fog over Lake Logan. They had not heard that a B-25 bomber was missing, and therefore didn't realize the plane was taking part in the search. But Roy knew right away that it was a P-38 fighter plane, because he had learned a lot from his cereal box airplane cards and cut-outs.

In Canton, Roy happily tagged along while his mother shopped throughout the morning. Then they ate lunch in the soda shop in the Trailways bus station, and when the afternoon rounds of shopping were done they topped off the day with a stop in Fullam's Ice Cream Parlor.

After finishing their ice cream, they walked to what was known as Hobo Corner, on Main Street near Rhinehart's Feed Store, and waited for the work bus to carry them home. The mill shift ended at 3:30 p.m., and it took several minutes for workers to board the bus and head out of town.

As Roy and his mother waited for the bus, they noticed that the rain clouds had parted to reveal a deep blue sky, the kind so familiar in late summer and autumn.

Then suddenly, something jarred the tranquil scene. "There was a ground-shaking roar," Roy recalled. "Then a large formation of military planes of various sizes roared overhead, so low I could see the numbers on their sides and 'U.S. Army' written underneath. It was a thrill for a nine-year-old mountain boy to witness such a thing in 1946."

A man who had been listening to the radio in Rhinehart's Store stepped out and said, "A bomber is down in these mountains."

*****

A LESSON WELL LEARNED

When Roy first heard that the B-25 crash site had been found, he listened to the description of the terrain, and he envisioned the plane sitting intact near the top of Cold Mountain. It was the most exciting thought he had had in a long time, and he was anxious to get a close look at the big bomber.

A short time later, he learned that five men had died on The Mountain, and the bomber was shattered into countless pieces. Then a feeling of sadness swept over him--but he still wanted to go to the scene.

He pleaded his case, but his father said "No," and nothing would change his mind.

Young Roy adored his uncle, Bob James, who died of injuries sustained in a car wreck that happened less than a week after he and his friends went to the B-25 crash site and had to struggle down Cold Mountain in the dark.

Roy was extemely upset by the news that his Uncle had died. And his feeling of sadness about the men on Cold Mountain grew deeper, and sharpened again with the death of his cousin, Henry Terrell, who died in a motorcycle accident only a few days after Bob James' funeral.

On the day of his Uncle's funeral at Fines Creek Baptist Church in Haywood County, Roy was not feeling well. He had eaten too many bananas with cream and sugar, a situation compounded by the winding two-lane road to the church.

By time for the funeral, he was too ill to go inside the sanctuary, so his mother allowed him to remain outside until the service was over.

While lying under a tree in the churchyard, pained by the loss of his Uncle Bob and sick at his stomach, Roy's innocent mind was also having to cope with his fresh knowledge of how fragile and uncertain human life can be. And he vowed then and there that he would get as much out of his own time on earth as possible. He would go places and do and see things and have lots of fun while he still had a chance.

But in the midst of mourning his Uncle, his unsettling new life-lesson, and his upset stomach, he was still trying to figure out some way he could get to see the remains of the B-25 bomber on Cold Mountain.

On the Sunday after the crash, a couple of his schoolmates came to Riverside Baptist Church carrying tow sacks. And after Sunday School and the morning worship service, they and their parents headed straight to The Mountain.

And at Cecil School the next day, those same classmates had an abundance of small parts from the plane to "show and tell."

Young Roy's feeling of being left out caused an ache in his heart, and he wanted to go to the crash site so badly that he even thought of sneaking off and going alone.

But he knew that his parents would be upset if their only child wandered off alone. And there were also other things to consider. He was aware that it was still "rattlesnake season," and he also thought of the stories he had heard about black panthers on Cold Mountain.

The local folks called panthers "painters," and they told of seeing the huge cats now and then and suspecting that they had come down from the heights and killed and eaten some some of their young livestock--baby goats, lambs, and newborn calves.

So Roy tried to stifle his longing to see what was left of the bomber by telling himself that if he never got a chance to see it, ever, at least his life would not be cut short by a rattlesnake bite, through becoming a nourishing meal for a painter, or maybe becoming lost forever on The Mountain.

Late autumn of 1946 ushered in plans for Thanksgiving and Christmas, and on the morning of December 25, Roy found something under his Christmas tree that helped take his mind off the B-25 bomber. It was a sturdy two-foot long scale model of an earth-hauling truck, as dandy as any boy could hope to receive.

The truck's splendid tires racked up hundreds of imaginary miles in the days and weeks that followed, and it wasn't long before every thought of the bomber crash on Cold Mountain left Roy's mind.

*****

MOVING ON DOWN THE ROAD

In the months following the bomber crash, Roy Moody's interest turned from his old familiar toys with wheels--to wheels on a bicycle. He received his first bike, and it provided a major thrust on the long path to his dream of driving a car down the gravel road to Canton.

And two years after the bomber crash, he and his parents moved on down the road, literally. They moved to the small town of Hazelwood, near Waynesville, which was much closer to Ned Moody's work at the Unagusta furniture plant.

Roy began classes at Hazelwood Elementary School, feeling very much the outsider. He longed to be back on Lake Logan Road, and he missed his chums at Cecil School terribly.

But after several months, he made friends and adjusted to his new surroundings. One of his new pals was a classmate named Ray Hogue. Later, when the two were students at Waynesville Township High School, they worked after school and on Saturdays at Ralph's Grocery Store in Hazelwood.

Ray Hogue joined the Air Force a month after he and Roy graduated from high school in 1955, and as years went by, they lost touch with each other.

But Ray would enter Roy's life again, in a remarkable way.

Since there was no money for college, Roy worked for the Winn-Dixie grocery store chain for a time after receiving his high school diploma. Then he joined the Army, completed training at Fort Benning, Georgia and served the rest of his tour of duty at Fort Knox, Kentucky, where he was his company's clerk.

After being honorably discharged, he worked for a year at the Ecusta paper mill in Pisgah Forest, near Brevard, N.C., and spent three years in the National Guard. And he began dating a pretty girl, Gail Paulette Penland of Candler, N.C., who was a student at Brevard Junior College.

To get to work each day, Roy drove or rode in a car pool down Highway 276 (Cruso Road) and passed by Cold Mountain--but his routine did nothing to jog his memory of the bomber crash and his great disappointment in not being able to visit the site.

*****

A FAMILY OF RACE FANS

Roy Moody and Gail Penland were married on August 18, 1961. And the young bride wholeheartedly joined her husband in attempting to get as much out of life as possible.

Since Gail was employed by Winn-Dixie stores, the couple had to plan their vacation time carefully, and since travel was tops on their agenda, they often drove all night to reach their destinations. And before they were able to buy a camper, they slept in their car.

After Roy's friend, Hilliard Jones, had convinced him to attend a stockcar race at the Asheville-Weaverville Speedway, he became an avid race fan.

As a spectator sport, auto racing was tailor-made for the boy who loved anything with wheels, and never outgrew it.

Roy and Gail's first son was born on May 5, 1967, and was named Curtis Roy Moody. His first name was in honor of Curtis "Crawfish" Crider, one of his parents' favorite racecar drivers. They first saw Crawfish in action at the Asheville-Weaverville Speedway. He was an independent driver, down-to-earth, and easily accessible to his many fans.

On September 27, 1970, the Moodys' second son was born. And he was named Cale DeWayne Moody, in honor of two of his parents' favorite NASCAR drivers, Cale Yarborough, who became a three-time NASCAR champion; and DeWayne "Tiny" Lund, whose wife, Wanda, was a native of the Crabtree section of Haywood County. The Lunds' only child, Christopher DeWayne Lund, called "Chris," was born the same year as little Cale DeWayne Moody.

Tiny Lund was a native of Iowa who operated a fish camp in Cross, South Carolina. His nickname was a twist on the fact that he was a very big man--6' 6'' inches tall and a rock-solid 270 pounds. And in 1963, the nation learned that Tiny was a mighty big man in other ways as well. He was awarded the *Carnegie Medal of Honor* for heroism in risking his own life to rescue fellow driver Marvin Panch from a burning sportscar.

While recovering from the accident, Marvin gave Tiny his blessing to drive his Wood Brothers-owned Ford in the 1963 Daytona 500--and Tiny won!.

He also won many short track races during his illustrious career.

In 1975, he was killed during a race at Talladega, Alabama.

His widow moved back to Haywood County, and later married Buddy Early. And Chris Lund and Cale Moody, the little boys with middle names honoring DeWayne "Tiny" Lund, formed a lasting friendship during their childhood years and graduated with the same class at Tuscola High School at Waynesville.

Roy and Gail Moody's other favorite racecar drivers were J.D. McDuffie of Sanford, N.C., who was killed during a Winston Cup race at Watkins Glen in New York State in August of 1991; and Henley Gray of Rome, Georgia.

They were independent drivers who operated on a tight budget, and by example taught Roy that he could travel to races far and wide on a shoestring. "I got a degree in economics from those two," he said.

After Roy's work at Ecusta, he gained employment closer to home, at the Champion Paper and Fibre Company plant in Waynesville.

And he and Gail continued to reap a ripe harvest of living, eventually traveling to beautiful and historic places in Canada and Mexico and all states except Hawaii and Alaska.

*****

A LOST MEMORY IGNITES

At NASCAR events, Roy often witnessed crashes. But while he vividly recalled details of his Uncle Bob James' death in a car wreck shortly after the B-25 bomber crash, neither that sorrowful event or wrecks on racetracks nudged Roy's recollection of the tragedy on Cold Mountain.

Nothing at all sparked his memory--until the fuse was lit by his two sons on a warm summer afternoon 32 years after the five World War II heroes died on The Mountain.

On a warm day in August of 1978, Curtis Moody, then age 11; and Cale, age 8, came home from Central Elementary School in Waynesville with reports of a grand outing. It had been "Library Day" at school, and the students visited the Haywood County Public Library. There, the youngsters were allowed to look at old copies of *The Mountaineer*, Haywood County's newspaper--on something they had never seen before.

It was called microfilm.

The Moody boys' eyes sparkled when they told Roy and Gail that they had even read the announcements that they had been born. "Daddy, you ought to go see it!" Cale urged. "You can read about lots of things that happened a long time ago."

That sounded right up Roy's alley, so he headed to the library as soon as he found some spare time. He picked the year 1946, thinking he might find the report of his Uncle Bob James's car wreck.

He threaded the microfilm, adjusted the focus, and started turning the knob.

Then suddenly, a headline almost leaped from the screen and hit him in the face like a bucket of ice water: BOMBER CRASHES ON COLD MOUNTAIN.

The words sent chills throughout his body, and in a mighty surge, the memory that had lain dormant for more than three decades exploded and hurled him into the past. It was September of 1946 all over again, and he was once again a nine-year-old boy watching the search planes over Canton, envying his schoolmates and their sacks of souvenir bomber parts, lying under the tree outside Fines Creek Baptist Church pondering the brevity of life and trying to figure out some way he could get to the bomber crash scene.

It was all as vivid in his mind as watching a movie on the big screen.

"I was stunned," Roy said. "And I couldn't believe I had forgotten such a major event."

He read the 1946 article three or four times. And by the time he left the library, his life had already taken a sharp turn down a new and never-to-be-forgotten path.

*****

A QUEST FOR THE PAST

Soon after the old news article shook Roy Moody's world, he made plans to find the bomber crash site. This time, he didn't need to have his father's permission--and in fact Ned Moody made plans to join his son on his quest.

In mid-October of 1978, they made their first attempt. In addition to Roy and Ned, the search party included Gail, Curtis, Cale, and the family's old dog, "Socks."

And it didn't take long for them to realize how difficult their task was going to be.

"We tried to go up the old Sorrells Creek trail below Camp Daniel Boone, because that's the way Dad always went to Cold Mountain," Roy said. "But after we got up a ways, we just ran out of trail."

So they backtracked and went to the Chambers Cove Road off Love Joy Road, where Roy's mother had spent her childhood years and had sweet memories of going huckleberry-picking on Cold Mountain. Her family took a horse and sled up a trail that Roy's father remembered well.

But again, the Moodys soon found that nature had blocked that path also.

Their second try, in late October, was made after Roy's friend, bear-hunter Louie Reece, told about Schoolhouse Branch logging road. The hikers followed that to a place where they could look down on the Dix Creek community and proceeded on the "Bus Body" logging road, so named because an old bus had been placed there long ago for use as shelter for loggers.

But the hikers soon suspected they had wandered onto the wrong trail, and since dusk was settling in fast, they gave up and got off The Mountain before dark.

When Roy told Louie Reece that they had become lost, Louie said he was going up the next day to look for bear tracks, and he would cut a notch in a prominent tree at the spot where they should leave the Schoolhouse Branch logging road and sort of pick their way across a steep ridge that would come out on one of the Cold Mountain Swags.

"Louie told us us to be careful and stay on the crest of the ridge," Roy recalled. "Veering to the left or right would result in being lost again."

This time, the family got all the way to their destination, but after searching diligently they were unable to find any sign of the B-25 bomber.

And so they gave up once more.

During the winter of 1978, Louie drew Roy a map detailing how to find the Plane Crash Trail, with instructions to "keep your eyes on the tall evergreen trees as you begin your climb from the Swag."

However, the Moodys made no attempt to find the crash site during the harsh winter months.

*****

AT LONG LAST

In April of 1979, Gail Moody was working a half day on Saturdays at Winn-Dixie, and one Saturday her car came screeching into the family's driveway, and she told Roy, "Let's hurry and get our stuff packed and head to Cold Mountain! I just *know* we're going to find the bomber crash!"

Roy's response was, "Are you crazy? It's way too late to start a hike up there!"

But Gail was not to be dissuaded. "Call your Dad." she said emphatically. "We are going."

When Ned Moody received the call, he said he wasn't willing to start a hike so late in the day, and advised, "You kids had better not go."

But go they did--and got to the Schoolhouse Branch road about 1 p.m. "I was uneasy," Roy recalled, "but we went right on without taking many breaks."

He said they made it in "record time" and kept their eyes on the evergreens, as Louie Reece had instructed.

"We went between the evergreens and picked up a small trail and started down," Roy said.

Eight-year-old Cale was walking ahead of the rest when he stopped and called out, "Dad! I found something!"

His discovery was a piece of electrical wire that was sticking out of the ground. Attached was some lettering, the name of a "Copper Corporation." And the date was 1944.

After finding the wire that was obviously from the B-25 bomber, the Moodys walked a little further into some extremely rough terrain.

Then suddenly, Roy spotted part of one of the bomber's wings. And down a little further were the two engines.

The feeling that came over him could not be adequately described in words. "Strange" was a close as he could come. It was a feeling that he was destined to visit that spot at that time, not a day earlier or later, and not until nearly 32 years had passed since Friday the 13th of September, 1946.

And he felt an unexplainable connection to the men who died at that spot on that day.

Gail Moody had known without a doubt that that April day was the time that they would find the bomber's remains. What she did not know was how it would impact the Moody family from that day forward.

After they all gathered some souvenirs, they had to come down Schoolhouse Branch road in the dark. They were exhausted--but also felt uplifted.

*****

LINKING TO WURTSMITH

The search for the remains of the bomber led Roy and Gail Moody into a new pastime. Along with their continuing interest in NASCAR, they took up mountain hiking.

Finally discovering the crash site increased Roy's interest in local history in general, and he enjoyed making contacts with former neighbors and friends who had been to the site soon after the tragedy. And he continued to collect all the printed material he could find about the crash.

In their travels, the Moodys had been to Michigan several times, but had not visited the state's Upper Peninsula. And plans were made for such a trip in July of 1983.

Shortly before time for that vacation, Roy was having breakfast at Hardee's restaurant in Waynesville, when in walked none other than his old friend from school days--Ray Hogue, who had recently retired from the Air Force with the rank of Captain.

And during his conversation with Roy, Captain Hogue was surprised to learn that Major General Paul B. Wurtsmith had been killed in the bomber crash on Cold Mountain. He remembered the crash, but didn't recall the names of the men who died.

Captain Hogue said he had visited Wurtsmith Air Force Base on a number of occasions through his duties as an aircraft inspector.

Roy was just as surprised by news of the Air Force Base as his friend had been about the death of General Wurtsmith, because Roy had no idea that a base in Michigan had been named for the General.

Captain Hogue urged Roy to visit the base, since it was on the route that he planned to travel during his upcoming vacation, and he also suggested that he take along some of his souvenirs from the crash site and copies of the news articles.

And he did.

After arriving in the small town of Oscoda, the Moodys checked into a nearby KOA Campground. "It was a beautiful place," Roy recalled. "Late that evening, Gail and I took a walk around the campground. A gentle breeze was blowing in the tall evergreens. I felt as though some supernatural force had drawn us there, and my mind wandered back to what happened on September 13, 1946 on Cold Mountain."

The next morning, they drove to the main gate of Wurtsmith Air Base where they read a sign proclaiming STRATEGIC AIR COMMAND (SAC) BASE--OFF LIMITS TO THE PUBLIC.

A Military Policeman immediately approached the Moodys' van and asked if they had business on the base. "No." Roy replied. "We just have some parts from the bomber General Wurtsmith was flying when he was killed, and we thought you folks might be interested."

The MP took the Moodys into a guard hut, and called the Base Commander. After explaining that the visitors had parts of General Wurtsmith's bomber, the MP smiled and turned to Roy and said, "He wants to know what in the world you're hauling them in."

After the MP informed the Commander that the parts could fit inside a desk drawer, the Moodys were told to stay put. A military escort would come for them shortly.

They were interviewed by Lieutenant Paul Turner, public affairs officer, and Sergeant Larry Dawson, the wing historian.

And the Moodys soon realized that they had more information about the bomber crash than those at the base.

It had been 37 years since the General had lost his life, and few servicemen who were stationed at Wurtsmith Air Force Base were even born when the bomber crashed on Cold Mountain.

Lieutenant Turner and Sergeant Dawson told the Moodys to have lunch and come back later. They wanted to bring in a reporter from the Oscoda newspaper and a crew from the local television station.

After the media interviews, Roy left copies of the *Waynesville Mountaineer* and *Asheville Citizen* articles about the crash, and he also left several small souvenirs from the bomber, including the piece of electrical wire that his son Cale had found five years earlier.

This took place on a Wednesday. A military parade was scheduled for Friday, and the Moodys were invited to participate in it.

"We thanked everyone, but declined to stay for the parade, since we had plans to continue on with our trip," Roy said. "And we later regretted not staying."

As soon as the couple returned home, a package was waiting for them. It was a brief biography and portrait of General Wurtsmith.

"I thought that was the end of it," Roy said. "There was nothing more I could learn about anything connected to the bomber crash."

And he added, "Wrong!"

In the years between 1983 and 1988, there seemed to be one news report after another that kept the Cold Mountain bomber crash foremost in Roy's mind. Among those reminders were: a B-25 being lifted from Lake Greenwood in South Carolina; a movie about a B-25 that crashed into the Empire State Building in 1945; a proposed lift of a B-25 from the Monongehela River at Pittsburgh; and a network TV news story about a KC-130 tanker that had crashed during a landing at Wurtsmith Air Force Base.

In addition, a man performing tests on behalf of a hearing aid company came to the Champion plant in Waynesville one day--and he was wearing a Wurtsmith Air Force Base jacket.

Roy said the man was surprised to learn that General Wurtsmith had died only a few miles away.

In addition, a number of people who had never been on Cold Mountain asked Roy to take them there.

And in the midst of the frequent reminders of September 13, 1946, Roy and Gail Moody continued enjoying their work, attending their sons' ball games and other school events, traveling, hiking, and going to NASCAR races--as happy as always.

*****

DARKNESS DESCENDS

In the early morning hours of New Year's Day, 1987, the Moodys' youngest son was involved in a minor auto accident in Waynesville. It was snowing at the time, and Roy and Gail got out of bed and helped get things settled concerning the mishap.

Roy returned to bed around 5 a.m. And when he woke up at 10 a.m., a change had come over his life. "I just didn't feel right," he said. It was a feeling that he couldn't quite describe, and one that he thought would soon pass.

Prior to that time, he had been exercising at the Champion Fitness Center in Canton, and he had noticed that he had begun to feel "washed out" after his sessions.

Roy thought he might have "mono" (mononucleosis), but when he had a medical checkup his blood tests and other areas of the exam showed nothing out of whack.

By the spring of 1988, he began having sleepless nights, and when not working at the plant, he would take long naps on his couch at home.

"I began to lose interest in all the things that had meant so much to me," Roy said. "I no longer wanted to travel, or hike or go to NASCAR races--or do anything else."

Gail Moody was puzzled and worried about her husband. "What's wrong with you?," she asked. "You were always so happy and enthusiastic about things. So what has happened to you?"

Roy had no answer for that.

The fact was, the little boy who lay under a tree in the Fines Creek Baptist churchyard and vowed to live life to the fullest, was now the man who didn't care if he lived or died.

And he didn't know what to do about it.

His wife didn't know either, but Roy later said with gratitude, "Gail stuck by me, trying to cheer me up and doing all the chores that I normally did, but had stopped doing. And she never complained."

During his bleak summer of 1988, Roy had a number of phone calls from a commodities broker who tried to convince him to invest in a "sure thing." He was in no mood to discuss the matter further, and when he answered his phone one day in August, the voice on the other end of the line sounded like the broker's.

Roy came close to hanging up on the caller, but then he realized the call was not what he had assumed.

*****

CAPTAIN STEELE CALLING

The man on the other end of the line was Captain Kent Steele, who was stationed at Wurtsmith Air Force Base.

Born in the farming country of northwest Ohio, Captain Steele was the youngest of four children in a devout Catholic family. After two years of college, he married and joined the Air Force. His first active duty assignment was at Wurtsmith Air Force Base. He continued his education through the military and became a Physician's Assistant.

Upon achieving PA status, he returned to Wurtsmith AFB as a Second Lieutenant, and in addition to his regular duties, he became involved in *Project Warrior*, a volunteer effort aimed at upgrading certain things at the base and preserving its history. And it was then that he discovered that very little information was available about Major General Paul B. Wurtsmith's life and untimely death.

Working with the Base Historian, he researched as much as he could and wrote some articles, and when he discovered what had been donated to the base by Roy Moody, his interest soared.

At the time of his contact with Roy, the Captain and his wife, Marti, had four children.

Their home in Michigan was an old farmhouse around three miles from the small town of Lincoln and some 20 miles from Wurtsmith Air Force Base. There, they had a large garden and kept goats to provide milk for the children.

However, Roy Moody learned nothing about the Captain's background during their initial phone conversation.

During that call, the Captain explained that he had come up with an idea after reading the news articles that Roy had left at the base. And that idea was to get the B-25 bomber engines off Cold Mountain and bring them to General Wurtsmith's native state and the Air Force Base that carried his name.

The engines could be refurbished and serve as a memorial to the General and the four men who died with him.

"Would you help us get the engines off Cold Mountain?," the Captain asked, unaware of the long black tunnel that Roy Moody was in at that time.

Roy couldn't have cared less about the bomber engines at that point, and he came up with a host of excuses why he couldn't assist in his caller's seemingly outlandish plan.

"I work swing shifts," Roy explained. "I have to work unexpected overtime when the situation calls for it. Getting the engines would take a long time, and I couldn't get off work that much."

Captain Steele persisted, "Please, Mr. Moody. We would love to have you help us."

And Roy quickly produced another litany of excuses: "It's impossible to get those engines off The Mountain. They're very hard to locate. The terrain is extremely rough. A truck can't get anywhere near the crash site. The engines are way too heavy for anyone to handle."

And the bottom line was--"If the engines could be moved off Cold Mountain, someone would have done it a long time ago."

But Captain Steele was buying none of it. "Mr. Moody, we can do it some way--if you will help us. O.K.?"

Reluctantly, Roy said that he would help. And when he got off the phone he said to himself, "What on earth have I gotten myself into?! Why did I say yes, when I feel the way I do?"

He dreaded the thought of what might lie ahead, and hoped that somehow the caller from Wurtsmith Air Force Base would change his mind.

His only consolation was that nothing would be required of him right away.

On that August day, he could not imagine that his life would soon take another dramatic turn, and that Captain Kent Steele would be one of several who would bring about the change.

*****

THE PROCESS BEGINS

In the afternoon of the same day he received the phone call from Captain Steele, Roy Moody was walking by the water-cooler at the Champion plant when he passed by Paul Allen, a co-worker and friend of some 30 years.

Paul paused and said, "Hey, Roy, come here. I've got something to say to you."

The two men stepped to one side, and Paul said, "Look, Roy, everybody in this plant has been noticing you for quite a while. You don't talk and laugh like you always did, and you drag around here like you're half dead."

If Roy had been able to experience any emotion, he would have been astonished by what came next. "I know exactly what's wrong with you," Paul continued. "You've got a bad case of what's called clinical depression. I had a relative who almost died because of it. And by the way, Roy, I've made an appointment for you with Lu Ann Webb and Pam Powlas tomorrow. So be there!"

Lu Ann and Pam were the "employee assistance personnel" at Champion Fitness Center in Canton, and Paul knew that they could start the ball rolling.

At the time, Roy didn't feel like keeping the appointment that his friend had made on his behalf.

But as he thought about the fact that Paul cared enough to try to help, and that he had told Captain Kent Steele that he would help with the bomber engine removal, he also thought about his childhood in the little house near Cold Mountain and in the modest home in Hazelwood, and the lessons he had learned along the way.

He had grown up poor, but was a millionaire in things that mattered most in life.

Roy's wife was one of seven children who had grown up on a small farm, and she too had been blessed with parents who provided a foundation for a good and honorable adult life.

And as Roy considered events of the past few days, he remembered one of the vital things his father had taught him. And the words came loud and clear in his mind: "Son, if you give a man your word--you keep it, even if it kills you."

He had given his word to Captain Kent Steele, and he knew he had to get a lot better in order to keep it.

So he followed through with the appointment that Paul Allen had made.

Later, he learned that Paul had a link to the B-25 bomber crash. He had visited the site not long after September 13, 1946--and had found a name tag that belonged to Master Sergeant Hosey W. Merritt.

Paul wanted to return it to the Merritt family, but didn't know how, and he later lost it.

It was yet another in the string of coincidences that seemed to be leading from the bomber crash to something "meant to be."

*****

SUNSHINE ONCE MORE

After Lu Ann Webb and Pam Powlas talked to Roy, they arranged for him to see Dr. Geraldine Powell in Asheville. And just as Paul Allen had said, the doctor's diagnosis was "clinical depression." Dr. Powell described it as "the closest to hell you can get while you're still on this planet."

Roy learned that the cause was a chemical imbalance in the brain, due to an insufficient amount of seratonin, a chemical that fires neurons which provide a sense of well-being.

And he learned that some of the causes of a drop in seratonin levels are heredity, stress, and sleep deprivation.

After visiting Dr. Powell, Roy looked back over his life and realized he had been driving himself too hard. He had been "burning the candle at both ends," perhaps in a subconscious effort to fulfill the pledge he made to himself in September, 1946, when he was that nine-year-old lad lying under a tree in the Fines Creek Baptist Churchyard and pondering the fleeting nature of human life.

As a young adult, Roy would stay up late, get up early, and work all day. But then, he wasn't bothered by having a small amount of sleep.

He remembered the many long trips he and Gail had made when they drove all day and all night and stayed up all the next day taking in a host of scenes and events. And when their sons were small, the trips were more difficult because they had to take along diapers, bottles, and everything else needed to care for an infant and small child on a long journey.

"We did this because we loved it," Roy said. "To us, it was a good kind of stress." (The couple left little Curtis and Cale in the care of Roy's parents only twice, when they went to California and Washington State.)

While in the Army, Roy pulled CQ (Charge of Quarters) duty two or three times a week, and during those times he got only two to four hours sleep.

As Roy later considered the severity of being in the throes of clinical depression, he wondered, "What if I hadn't taken Cale's advice and looked at old newspaper copies on microfilm? What if Ray Hogue hadn't walked into Hardee's restaurant and told me about Wurtsmith Air Force Base? What if I had hung up the phone and hadn't told Captain Steele I'd help with the bomber engines? And what if Paul Allen hadn't made an appointment for me, and ordered me to keep it?

If none of that had happened, the outcome of his clinical depression might have ended in genuine tragedy for him and his family.

And the chain of events, of course, all went back to the foggy day in 1946 when the B-25 bomber crashed on Cold Mountain, and his childhood longing to see the big plane.

All links of the chain had led a desperate man to a place where the dense fog of his life was about to lift and his storm clouds were about to part and reveal blue sky once more.

Dr. Powell prescribed a medication, *Pamelor*, for Roy, with a caution that it might or might not work. It would be a hit-or-miss kind of situation until something was found that was effective.

But Dr. Powell soon noted that Roy had one of the worst cases of clinical depression she had ever seen--and also made one of the swiftest recoveries.

The initial medication worked wonders, and in less than a month he was beginning to feel more like his old self again.

He shared his story here in the hope that those who may recognize the signs of clinical depression in themselves or others will know that it doesn't have to be that way.

"Don't be afraid to admit that something is wrong," he urged. "Seek help right away!"

*****

MEMORIALS FROM THE BOMBER

Not long after Roy started on the road to recovery, he was traveling down Highway 276 at Cruso, and he remembered that one of the big tires from the bomber had been rolled off The Mountain by several youths shortly after the crash, and it had been resting near the creek on the Norris property since 1946.

He wasn't thinking about his beloved old Goodyear tire that vanished when he was a little boy, but something deep in his mind may have urged him to try to keep the same thing from happening to the old bomber tire.

It was an important piece of history.

Roy turned onto the Old Michal Road, and immediately saw a FOR SALE sign in the yard of the Norris homeplace.

Tom Norris, who was startled by the bomber when it passed over his house in 1946, had died many years earlier, as had his wife. And their son Bill Norris and his wife, Wales, who lived at the homeplace, had also passed on.

When Roy drove up in his truck, several women were standing in the yard, including Bill and Wales' daughter, Joyce Norris Mease, and Joyce's daughter Linda.

Roy asked about plans for the B-25 tire, and was told that a decision had not yet been made. The women told Roy if he would like to have the tire, it would be fine with them, but he should first discuss it with Bill Norris' son, Hoyt.

A few days later, Hoyt Norris told Roy he'd be glad to let him have the tire, if O.C. Chambers, who had helped roll it off Cold Mountain in 1946, didn't want to keep it.

Roy's main interest was simply that the tire be preserved, and his opinion was that O.C. should be the one to have it. And when asked, O.C. said yes, he'd like to keep the old souvenir.

The B-25 tire, which showed no sign of wear after so many decades in all kinds of weather, was mounted in the back yard at the home of O.C. and his wife, Doris, on Meadow Grove Church Road, near Cruso Road, where there is a clear view of Cold Mountain and the site of the bomber crash.

Lined directly with the site, the tire is a memorial to the five heroes who died there.

And decades after the crash, the lawn at the home of William J. "Bill" and Wilhelmina Rhodarmer near Canton became the site of another memorial. The rim of the tire Bill and his buddies rolled off The Mountain in 1946 became a planter filled with flowers each spring.

The propeller from the B-25, which was brought down Cold Mountain by Boy Scouts, mounted and stored in the Scout Room of Canton's First United Methodist Church for decades, was later donated to the Canton Museum.

In 1988, Roy Moody, right, was pictured with the B-25 tire mounted on the back lawn at the home of O.C. Chambers, second from right. Others pictured are, left to right, Frank Chambers and Ned Norris, who helped O.C. roll the tire off Cold Mountain in 1946, when they were teenagers. The fourth tire-roller, J.V. Plemmons, was not available for the photo. (Mountaineer photo by Terri Crook.).

In the spring of 2004, white petunias were the flowers chosen for the B-25 bomber tire rim serving as a memorial planter at the home of Bill Rhodarmer, right, near Canton. As teenagers in 1946, Bill and Robert Fisher, left, and their friend Stuart Smathers (deceased at the time of this photo) rolled the tire off Cold Mountain.. John H. "Johnny" Rhodarmer Jr., center, accompanied Bill to the crash site three days later. (Photo by Wilhelmina Rhodarmer.)

GROUNDWORK FOR LIFT-OFF

After O.C. Chambers had mounted the old bomber tire in his yard, Roy Moody began wondering if he would ever hear from Captain Kent Steele again.

He thought his discouraging words during their earlier phone conversation might have caused the officer to abandon his idea of lifting the bomber engines off Cold Mountain.

If he had known Captain Steele a little better then, he would have realized that nothing would discourage him. His mind was made up, and that was that.

And one Sunday morning in early November of 1988, the phone rang at the Moody residence. It was the Captain, and he asked if Roy could come meet him at the Holiday Inn at the Highway 276 and Maggie Valley Road intersection near Waynesville.

It was drizzling rain that day, and when Roy met the Air Force officer he was a bit surprised. He had envisioned an administrative type in dress uniform, and he assumed he had spent a comfortable night in the motel.

However, greeting Roy in the motel lobby was a man wearing camouflage fatigues and boots, a man who had spent the cold night in the back of his truck at the Tennessee-North Carolina Welcome Center.

Captain Steele was not a tall man, and he had a youthful "boy next door" look. But Roy soon learned that his last name fit him perfectly. He was a "Man of Steel" in every sense of the word.

"And no one could have been nicer," Roy added.

The Captain, who was on his way back to Wurtsmith Air Force Base after a desert training session in Texas, asked Roy to ride along in his truck and show him the foot of Cold Mountain and the various roads leading to it.

And around 1 o'clock that afternoon, the Captain asked Roy if he could take him to the top of The Mountain and let him get a look at the bomber engines.

Roy was apprehensive about that request, and he replied that it was almost too late to go, and that they might have to come down in the dark

But they went on up a logging road as far as the Captain's truck would go, and by that time the drizzling rain was turning to snow.

"I was sure hoping Captain Steele would want to turn back, but he didn't," Roy recalled. So they ate some military rations and started hiking, with the Captain carrying a very heavy pack of photographic equipment.

"The closer we got to the crash site, the harder it snowed," Roy said. "I had never been in snow coming down that hard in my life, and it was getting deep." The situation was becoming alarming.

Roy told the Captain that they had to keep on the ridge and not veer right or left, and he stressed, "If we don't keep on the ridge, we could freeze to death up here!" And he wasn't kidding.

The two men then made their way down the steep Mountain face and were barely able to locate the engines under the mounting snow.

Captain Steele filmed the engines location and surrounding terrain, and recorded comments. All would be presented to his Base Commander, who would have to give permission for the engines to be brought to Michigan.

When the filming was completed, it was growing dark and the men could barely see each other through the blizzard. "Hold onto my belt," Roy told the Captain as they began to inch their way back to the truck. The parking lights had been left on, and when their dull gleam became visible, nothing could have been more beautiful.

The two had had a harrowing experience, to say the least.

Captain Steele spent the night with the Moodys, and told of his many fascinating experiences. And he also gave them a little lesson in nutrition, saying a person doesn't need more than pinto beans or "pork'n beans" to keep going strong in a tight situation.

When he said goodbye the next day, Roy and Gail knew that, in spite of his terrible experience on Cold Mountain, they had not seen the last of "The Man of Steel."

And they also knew they had made a friend they would treasure forever.

"I'll be back with a crew around April 1," the Captain said.

*****

In early April of 1989, Haywood County received a spring snow, and some was still lingering on the ground when Captain Steele called Roy Moody again, and said he was coming to get the bomber engines. He would be accompanied by a female Captain, two Lieutenants, and two Airmen from Wurtsmith Air Force Base.

They would bring a three-quarter-ton truck, winches, pulleys, metal detectors, and other equipment.

Roy and Gail had earlier invited them to stay at their house, and Captain Steele said they would bring six cots to sleep on in the Moody's basement. But Roy told him, "No way! Forget the cots. We've got enough beds and fold-out couches in places for all of you to rest well."

Then the Captain said he would bring plenty of military rations for himself and the crew. But Roy told him to forget that too. Gail had insisted on cooking for them all.

Captain Steele expressed his gratitude for the kind offers, and on Saturday, April 7, he called again to say he and his assistants were leaving Wurtsmith Air Force Base around 3 a.m. Sunday morning and would complete the 800 mile journey some time Sunday night. The two lieutenants would not be coming because of family emergencies.

Captain Steele, Captain Theda Furlonge, Airman John McCann, and Airman Mike Montgomery reached the Moody residence in Waynesville about 10 p.m. Sunday, April 8.

"Captain Steele came to the door," Roy recalled, "and I don't think I've ever seen a more tired-looking man. They were all ready for bed, for sure."

An attractive 38-year-old African-American, Captain Furlonge was a dynamic woman with a fine sense of humor. "She was a lot of fun," Roy said.

She said that when the group began going up the Interstate-40 Gorge and she got a good look at the mountains, she knew they were in for "no vacation."

Captain Furlonge had grown up in the Bronx in New York City. She was the personnel officer at Wurtsmith Air Force Base, and she was also an animal-lover who brought her little dog on the trip.

Airman McCann was around 20-years-old and was from Pawtucket, Rhode Island, where his family owned a hardware store. He said Gail Moody reminded him of his mother.

Yukon, Oklahoma was the hometown of Airman Montgomery, who was also around age 20.

"They were all nice as could be," Roy said. No one could have asked for better guests.

Roy was working the 3-to-11 p.m. shift during the week the Wurtsmith personnel were in Haywood County, so he was able to help them during the morning hours.

On the first day, Monday, Roy took the group to the old Michal Farm off Cruso Road and from there they attempted to find a trail they could follow to Cold Mountain. Roy had to leave after a while, and Captain Steele and the others went on to explore that side of The Mountain in an effort to determine if there was a feasible way to use a winch or bring the engines down on a sled.

On Tuesday, Roy took Captain Steele and Airman McCann up the Schoolhouse Branch logging road. Jerry Burke, a local resident who knew The Mountain well, and Raymond Temple, the Champion plant's security guard at Lake Logan, also accompanied them up the road.

The two servicemen planned to come down The Mountain from the crash site and pick up Lenoir Creek to see if they could locate some kind of trail which would allow the engines to be sledded down.

Captain Theda Furlonge and Airman Mike Montgomery were to go to the Michal Farm and wait for them there with the Air Force truck--and just be there in case their help was needed.

Around 10 o'clock that night, Roy Moody was nearing the end of his shift at the plant in Waynesville when he received a phone call. It was Captain Steele.

"Roy, don't be upset," the Captain began, "but I've somehow lost Theda and Mike. They were not at the Michal Farm when John and I came out."

Roy's heart almost stopped.

"How can I not be upset?!," he thought. "There's no telling where they are, or how we'll find them! What if they decided to go up Cold Mountain and have gotten lost in the dark?!"

Roy figured they might be in for an all-night search, or worse.

But when he got home around 11:15 p.m., he was greatly relieved to see the entire Wurtsmith crew sitting in his living room, looking at maps and talking about where they had been.

Captain Furlonge explained that Captain Steele and Airman McCann were taking so long to get off The Mountain that she and Airman Montgomery decided take the Air Force truck and do a little sightseeing in the area in the late afternoon.

They stopped at a sawmill on Highway 276, and Captain Furlonge asked where she might be able to find a jar of genuine "mountain moonshine." She wanted to take it back to the Wurtsmith Air Force Base and display it as a souvenir on her desk in the Personnel Office.

A man at the sawmill said he could have some moonshine for her by late Friday--but the crew was due to head back to the base before then, so Captain Furlonge gave up that idea.

She inquired about how to get to the home of the man who had one of the B-25 bomber tires mounted in his yard, and then she and Airman Montgomery went back to the Michal Farm and waited some more. After a while, they decided to go to O.C. Chambers' house.

When Captain Steele and Airman McCann came off The Mountain that night, Captain Furlonge and Airman Montgomery were deep in conversation with the man who had helped roll the tire off Cold Mountain in 1946.

After talking to Roy on the phone, Captain Steele had an idea they might be at the Chambers house, and a nice woman near the Michal Farm took him and Airman McCann there in her car.

When Roy arrived home that night, he found that Captain Steele was learning a lot more about the validity of the excuses he had given him when he was trying to get out of helping with the engine removal. The bad experience he had had in the November blizzard on The Mountain had not caused them to sink in--but his ventures on that day in April of 1989 had indeed given them credence.

"You told me right, Roy," Captain Steele said. "Cold Mountain is rougher than I ever thought. We almost failed to locate the engines. The snow was waist deep up there, and coming down there was no trail--just rock cliffs and caves that looked like bear dens. We're due back at the base by Friday night. I don't know what we're going to do."

But "The Man of Steel" was not about to give up. He said he and his crew would go back and look around again on Wednesday and see what they could come up with.

*****

The next day, O.C. Chambers caught up with Roy Moody at work, and told him the Wurtsmith Air Base crew was back at his house that morning, and appeared to be very discouraged.

He said he offered to give them his bomber tire, because they were such good folks and he hated for them to have to go back to Michigan empty-handed after all their efforts.

However, Captain Steele told O.C. that the tire should remain mounted on his lawn, since it was a fitting memorial in a perfect spot facing Cold Mountain.

Other kinds of wheels were turning in the Captain's head, and he soon went back to the Moody residence and got on the phone to various military personnel. A vital source was Army National Guard Sergeant Jim Stanley of Murphy, North Carolina, who put him in touch with a helicopter unit in Raleigh.

The Raleigh unit was required to made one lift per month, and it so happened that one had not been made in April.

The pieces were beginning to come together.

Officials of the Champion plant gave permission for a National Guard Black Hawk helicopter to land at the Lake Logan air strip.

Thursday was a hectic day, with Captain Steele continuing to pull strings hither and yon. Turning to Roy, he said, "I need you. Can you get off work this afternoon?"

Roy had some personal holidays left for the year, and he called the plant and received permission to take one.

Word came from the Major in charge of the National Guard unit in Raleigh that he could have a helicopter at Cold Mountain by lunchtime, and he told Captain Steele to have some Kentucky Fried Chicken waiting at Lake Logan, since the crew would not have time for lunch prior to the trip.

Major Terry Benson and CW4 Randy Watkins would be the helicopter pilots, and the master loader would be Specialist Fourth Class Roger Jones. Sergeant Jim Stanley would come to assist with ground radio communications. He would also help with loading the engines for lift-off, as would Airmen McCann and Montgomery.

Captain Steele told Roy and Captain Furlonge to get to the nearest Kentucky Fried Chicken restaurant on the double and then head for the Lake Logan airstrip. "By then, we were on the ragged edge for time," Roy said.

Captain Steele and Airmen McCann and Montgomery hurried on to Lake Logan.

*****

A MEDIA EVENT

Roy said he couldn't believe his eyes when he and Captain Furlonge delivered the fried chicken. The place was swarming with local citizens and news media--a crew from *WLOS-TV* in Asheville and reporters Don Leavenworth of the *Asheville Citizen-Times* and Terri Crook of *The Mountaineer* in Waynesville.

Many of the faces were familiar to Roy from his childhood years in the area.

Reporter Leavenworth button-holed him for an interview, and Captain Steele said, "Make it quick, Roy. They want you to be up at the end of that logging road in your truck, so you can bring out some of the helicopter crew. They may have to hike out to you, in case something goes wrong up there."

The Captain gave Roy a walkie-talkie radio so he could stay in touch, and after the brief interview he got behind the wheel of his truck and was off.

As he drove alone up the logging road, his mind flashed back to his days at Cecil School, his pals at Riverside Baptist Church with their tow sacks ready to gather souvenirs from the bomber, the search planes roaring over Canton.

And a horrible thought leaped into his mind.

He remembered that the day was the 13th of April, 1989! Thank goodness it was a Thursday instead of a Friday! It surely would not end like that long ago Friday the 13th of September, when the bomber engines had become cold and silent on Cold Mountain.

Roy prayed that nothing would go wrong.

At the end of Schoolhouse Branch logging road, he radioed back to Captain Steele and told him he had arrived at his station.

Shortly thereafter, a Black Hawk helicopter churned the air over Roy's head on its way to The Mountain. And before long there were indications that something indeed might go wrong.

"The chopper hovered over Cold Mountain for a few minutes, and left," Roy recalled. It turned out that the cable was too short and in order to take care of the problem it landed in a hay field near Frank Blaylock's *Up the River General Store* on Cruso Road.

After members of the ground crew were safely lowered to the site of the bomber crash, the helicopter left again and sat down in the hay field to wait for word that the engines had been secured for the lift-off.

Then, after what seemed to be a long time, Roy saw the helicopter heading for Cold Mountain again, and this time it hovered over the crash site for quite a while.

But then its engines revved up again and it flew off into the distance. Time passed, and Roy lay down in his truck, thinking he might as well catch a short nap. But soon Captain Steele's anxious voice came crackling through the radio, "What's going on up there, Roy? It's getting close to six o'clock!"

Roy radioed back that he had no idea what was going on.

"It was very quiet up there," he recalled, and then he heard the heart-thumping sound of the helicopter again--heading back to The Mountain. Because it had taken so long to get the cargo hooked just right for lift-off, the chopper had run low on fuel and had to go to Asheville to get more.

This time, the magnificent whirlybird perched over the crash site for several minutes. Then Roy saw it weave and pitch above its tremendous load, and it was up and away, with the two B-25 engines in a huge cargo net.

Roy radioed Captain Steele, "They're coming right over me with the engines now!" He could see the engines plainly, and they appeared to be much too low! They were right over his head--and then in the distance he could see the helicopter approaching a mountain top before reaching the Lake Logan airstrip. Everything still looked far too low, and Roy prayed as hard as he could: "Dear Lord, please don't let this be another disaster!"

Just as Roy Norris had done on September 13, 1946, Roy Moody looked at his watch. It was 6:15 p.m.

But Roy soon let out a sign of relief. "Thank God, the helicopter crew knew exactly what it was doing, and all went well," he said.

Captain Steele soon radioed Roy and told him to head on back down The Mountain. He said the helicopter would drop off the engines and go back to pick up the loading crew. And he added that Captain Theda Furlonge was going to get her wish to ride in the chopper over Cold Mountain.

On the way back to Lake Logan, Roy's friend Paul Woody came rushing out of his house to tell him the story had been on the 6 o'clock news on WLOS-TV. But because the operation had taken so much longer than expected, the reporter and camera crew had to miss the grand finale.

Back at "ground zero," Roy had the pleasure of talking to many of his former schoolmates and other friends and neighbors from his cherished childhood years on Lake Logan Road.

It had been a day for all to remember.

Raymond Temple, Jerry Burke, and others assisted in freeing the cargo from the net. The engines' tremendous weight required a Champion plant front-end loader, operated by Hershel Owens Jr., for placement in the Air Force truck.

Several other smaller bomber parts were also loaded, and when they were ready to roll, the back of the truck almost dragged the ground.

*****

Since the National Guard helicopter unit would have had to make an April airlift anyway, the project had been completed with no cost to taxpayers other than use of the Air Force truck. Even the gas for the trip to and from Michigan was paid for by volunteers.

*****

Pictured in the Moody home after the bomber engines were lifted off Cold Mountain were, left to right, Captain Theda Furlonge, Captain Kent Steele, Airman Mike Montgomery, Sergeant Jim Stanley, and Airman John McCann.

The morning after the airlift, Friday, April 14, 1989, Gail Moody awakened her guests from Wurtsmith Air Force Base at 5 a.m. and served them breakfast. And then they said their goodbyes and were off on their 800 mile journey with their unusual cargo.

Just as they had arrived in Haywood County a week earlier, they would be exhausted at the end of the trip. But they would also feel uplifted--just as Roy and Gail Moody had felt when they came down from Cold Mountain after locating the bomber wing and engines 11 years earlier.

However, it was discovered that the bomber engines were in much worse condition than they appeared when observed in the spots where they had lain for decades on Cold Mountain. But Captain Steele felt that he might be able to break them down and construct one engine from the good parts. He would give it his best shot as a volunteer in his off-duty hours.

*****

The day after the engines airlift was Roy Moody's regular day off work, and he spent it answering his phone, which rang almost constantly. The news of the airlift had spread far and wide. People who remembered him from his childhood days, old friends, acquaintances, and people he had never met called to talk about the event, and about the bomber crash in 1946. Some callers had been to the scene of the crash shortly after it happened.

On the Sunday after the airlift, Roy and Gail came home from Hazelwood Baptist Church to find a stranger waiting in their front yard. And he turned out to be a very interesting fellow.

His name was Dwight McCarter, and he lived near Pigeon Forge, Tennessee. He was a backwoods ranger with the Great Smoky Mountains National Park Service, and search-and -rescue was part of his job.

His hobby was looking for wreckage of planes that crashed in the Smoky and Blue Ridge mountains many years ago.

Through the years, he had taken approximately 900 photos--all angles of old plane wrecks and the scenes surrounding them in the Smokies.

During the week of the B-25 engines airlift from Cold Mountain, he had been searching for the remains of the C-78 Cessna which crashed near Maggie Valley in 1943. He noted that two Navy pilots on board had picked up an enlisted man at one of their stops, and because there was not an extra parachute for the unfortunate passenger, he had to ride the crippled plane on down and was killed. The two pilots parachuted out over Maggie Valley and survived.

The body of the enlisted man was sledded down the mountain and emerged at the foot of where Maggie Valley's *Ghost Town* tourist attraction was established a decade later.

After discussing the Cold Mountain bomber crash with the Moodys, the backwoods ranger said he'd like to hike up Cold Mountain at some point, even though no major parts of the plane remained at the site. But on that Sunday, he needed to get on with his main mission.

So Gail Moody fortified him with two hotdogs, and he continued on his quest. Before he returned to Tennessee, he did locate the remains of the 1943 crash, and commented, "That was some of the roughest terrain I'd ever been in!"

Several months later, Dwight McCarter called Roy and reported that he had been looking for the remains of plane carrying the three men and 25,000 baby chicks--the 1947 crash that had been found by bear-hunters Beanie Moody and Jack Frady.

He said that in searching for that old crash, he had become totally lost in the mountains for several days.

Several years after he visited Roy and Gail Moody, Dwight McCarter retired from the Park Service, and with Jeff Wadley, a Lieutenant Colonel with the Tennessee Civil Air Patrol who served as a mission coorinator and trainer in the Smokies, he co-authored a book about 52 airplane crashes in the Great Smoky Mountains National Park from the 1920s to 2000. (The B-25 bomber crash on Cold Mountain was not included in the book, because it did not occur in the Smokies.)

Titled *Mayday! Mayday!*, the Watley-McCarter book was published by the University of Tennessee Press in 2002.

Dwight McCarter is also author of an earlier book titled *Lost!--A Ranger's Journal of Search and Rescue in the Great Smoky Mountains National Park*, published in 1998.

*****

OFF TO ALASKA

Captain Kent Steele had barely had time to rest from his April, 1989 expedition to Cold Mountain when he had unexpected news.

He received order of transfer to an Air Force Base in Alaska, and was to be there without delay.

His wife, Marti, and the couple's children stayed in Michigan until their house and land was sold.

(By 2005, the Captain had retired from the Air Force, but was still in Alaska. After leaving Michigan, the Steeles had three more children and adopted three Vietnamese orphans--making a total of 10. They bought a farm in Alaska, and Captain Steele continued as a Physician's Assistant working in village clinics and oilrigs throughout the state, and in medical missions to Southeast Asia.)

Captain Theda Furlonge had invited Roy and Gail Moody to visit Wurtsmith Air Force Base again and stay at her home, and a month after the engines were lifted from Cold Mountain they took some vacation time and headed to Michigan.

"Captain Furlonge had a beautiful house right on Lake Huron," Roy said, "and we spent one night with her."

The next day, they went to the Steele farm, and were warmly welcomed for an overnight stay by the Captain's wife and four children. A fifth child was on the way by then.

Early the next morning, the Moodys received a call from Captain Furlonge, who told them if they could get back to Oscoda by 9 a.m. they could tour Wurtsmith Air Force Base along with a group of foreign dignitaries.

The Moodys made haste, and were able to see how pilots were trained. They went inside B-52 bombers, KC-130 refueling tankers, and saw other things of great interest.

It more than made up for not taking part in the parade at the base in 1983.

Before they had left for Michigan, Roy told his parents that he'd like to look up General Wurtsmith's brother, Frank, in Detroit. But his father's advice was not to do it, because it might stir up painful memories.

So the Moodys went on into Canada and came home without contacting the General's kin.

That summer, however, Roy received a card from Frank Wurtsmith and his wife, Shirley, thanking him for his interest in General Wurtsmith. And they invited the Moodys to visit them whenever possible.

So in September of 1989, the Moodys made another trip to Michigan and visited the couple.

The Wurtsmith's had a large box of photos which they showed Roy and Gail--young Paul Wurtsmith as an altar boy at Holy Redeemer Church, as a teenager working on his Model-T hotrod, and other images from a life destined for greatness and a too-early death.

Roy told the couple all he had learned about the crash, about Cold Mountain and the warm-hearted people who lived near it, and how the crash had impacted his own life.

"I'd give anything if I had a tape recorder to record all this." Shirley Wurtsmith said.

And during their conversation, she shared some of her personal history. She said she had been suffering from clinical depression, and was much better--after taking *Pamelor*--the same medication that brought Roy out of his long inner midnight.

It was another coincidence among the mounting numbers connected to September 13, 1946 on Cold Mountain.

The Wurtsmiths said they would like to stop in Haywood County sometime, while on their way to Florida, and visit the Moodys and get a good look at Cold Mountain.

But it was not to be.

For several years after their visit in Detroit, Roy and Gail received cards from the couple at Christmas, and then no more.

(Frank Wurtsmith died on August 11, 2001, and Shirley died on January 6, 2003.)

Gail Moody, center, is pictured with Shirley Wurtsmith and her husband, Frank, brother of General Paul B. Wurtsmith, in the couple's home in Detroit.

After visiting the Wurtsmiths, Roy and Gail traveled on to Sherwood, Ohio. It was not far from the Michigan border and was the native territory of Captain Kent Steele.

There, they had the privilege of getting to know all members of the Captain's family who were still living in the area. "Like everyone else I had met in connection with the bomber crash, they were wonderful people," Roy said.

Captain Steele's sister, Lee Ann Fritch, a teacher; and her husband, Larry, who was employed by the huge General Motors plant in Sherwood, were genial hosts, and the Moodys visited them during three of their vacations in later years.

In turn, the Fritches spent a week with the Moodys in Waynesville during a General Motors strike.

Larry Fritch owned many acres of farmland, and one afternoon Roy rode with him to check on his crops. As the two sat gazing over the flourishing fields of Ohio summer, Larry turned to his guest with a pensive look on his face, and said, "You know, Roy, if that bomber hadn't crashed on Cold Mountain, we wouldn't be sitting here looking at my soybeans."

The ripples of fate had indeed spread from The Mountain to unusual places and circumstances.

*****

A SAD FAREWELL

Not long after Captain Kent Steele was transferred to Alaska, many personnel from Wurtsmith Air Force Base, including Captain Theda Furlonge, were sent to Saudi Arabia to prepare for B-52 operations in the Gulf War. The year was 1990.

During that era, America's awesome military power brought about many changes in the world. The Cold War between America and the Soviet Union came an end, and the United States Congress began cutting back military spending.

It was said that Wurtsmith Air Force Base became "a victim of its own success" as a mighty part of the Stragetic Air Command. As a result of a disarmament pact signed by the United States and Soviet Union, the base was one of 30 targeted for closing. The unwelcome word came down in April of 1991.

The final military air show at the base featured the famed *Thunderbirds* on June 30, 1992. And on December 15, 1992, the last B-52 bomber, fondly called the *Old Crow Express*, thundered off the Wurtsmith runway for the last time.

To say the occasion was a sad one would be a gross understatement.

The Old Crow Express joined other old B-52s in a scrap yard in Arizona, where they were cut up by workers functioning under the new Arms Limitation Agreement.

The unexpected transfer of Captain Kent Steele to Alaska, the Gulf War, which drew so many troops from Wurtsmith Air Force Base; and finally the news that the base was to be closed brought an end to the Project Warrior volunteer operations.

Just as no one could have foreseen the B-25 crash on Cold Mountain, no one could have predicted what would happen to troops at Wurtsmith Air Base, and to the base itself.

Although it became impossible for the bomber engines to fulfill the intended mission in 1989, they nevertheless served an honorable purpose in being returned to the state where General Paul B. Wurtsmith was born and spent the years of his youth before World War II, the state where he served as a pilot in the early days of his stellar career--and the state where the B-25 engines were revved up for the final flight which ended on Cold Mountain in 1946.

In early 1993, the closing of Wurtsmith Air Force Base was competed--40 years after it was renamed in honor of the General who died at age 40.

Those who served at Wurtsmith Air Force Base through its long and distinguished history have cherished memories of the experience, and many of their thoughts are posted on the *Wurtsmith Air Force Base Historical Preservation* web site on the Internet.

After the base closing, its runway became the Oscoda-Wurtsmith Airport. Thousands of visitors come each year to the nearby *Yankee Air Museum*, which is devoted to preservation of old aircraft and the history of Wurtsmith Base.

In the Museum, a special section honoring Major General Paul B. Wurtsmith contains a piece of the B-52 bomber lifted from Cold Mountain. It is displayed in a glass case beneath a large oil portrait of the General. The bomber piece was donated to the Museum by Captain James S. Johnson of Nashville, Tennessee, an airline pilot who lived in Brevard in the late 1960's and early 1970's.

A piece of the B-25 bomber wreckage lifted from Cold Mountain is displayed beneath a portrait of General Paul B. Wurtsmith in a special section of the Yankee Air Museum at Oscoda, Michigan. (Photo courtesy of Colonel James B. McLaughlin)

The Museum is operated by a committee from the approximarely 100 volunteer members of the Yankee Air Force, Colonel James B. McLaughlin, chairman.

At the time of this book's publication, Museum hours were 11 a.m. to 3 p.m. Fridays, Saturdays, and Sundays, from May through October each year. Fly-ins were held annually.

*****

WRONG AGAIN

After Wurtsmith Air Force Base was closed, Roy Moody gathered all his photos and papers pertaining to the B-25 bomber crash, put them away, and told his wife that that chapter of his life was probably closing also.

But like so many other times when he thought there was nothing else to learn, or do, about what happened on September 13, 1946 on Cold Mountain--he was wrong again.

One day in the mid-1990s, Roy had a call from O.C. Chambers, who told him he had had a visit by the son of one of the men who died on Cold Mountain. Roy had been away on vacation at that time.

The visitor was Richard Oakley.

So Roy's interest in the bomber crash was fired anew. He made a call to the Oakley residence, and when the voice of the son of Lieutenant Colonel Paul R. Okerbloom came on the line, he had almost as many chills as when he ran across the microfilm story about the crash on Cold Mountain. "I felt like I was talking to a ghost," he said.

Roy told the former "Dickie" Okerbloom about the difficulty of getting to the crash site, but that he'd be glad to take him there, show him around the area, and introduce him to some of its fine residents.

Later, Richard Oakley called the Moody residence, and Roy had chills again. The call came while Roy was watching a documentary about B-25 bombers.

The son of Colonel Okerbloom made plans to return to Haywood County after his initial visit, but as stated earlier, something interferred.

"I hope he can come in the future," Roy said.

*****

MEN AND MOUNTAIN MOVE ON

By spring of 2004, it had been several years since Roy Moody had made a hike to the site of the B-25 crash, and his friend, Captain Ray Hogue, had never been and wanted to go. So the two former schoolmates and Gay Calhoun and Mack Ledbetter set out for Cold Mountain early one sunny morning in May.

Captain Ray Hogue was pictured at his home prior to his hike to the bomber crash site in May, 2004. .

Roy Moody, Mack Ledbetter, and Gay Calhoun, left to right, were captured by Captain Ray Hogue's camera during an "oatmeal-cake and water break" on their hike up Cold Mountain.

All four hikers were military veterans, and senior citizens.

Gay Calhoun was 81-years-old at that time, but could out-hike most men less than half his age. Like the men who died on Cold Mountain, he had served in the Army Air Force during World War II, and he was familiar with the function of B-25 bombers.

When the four men reached the Cold Mountain Swag, Roy Moody was shocked by the changes nature had wrought.

The center of the Swag, which had been a smooth grassy meadow through so many decades, had grown up with beech trees, laurel, and tangles of other plant life.

The men had no trouble finding the bomber crash area, although it too had changed greatly.

The main clue was a large hardwood tree that had stood near where the bomber engines had lain. Before 2004, the tree had become uprooted, with an exposed root mass as tall as the ceiling of a room in an average home. And therefore it still served as a good marker for those seeking the site.

In its own way, the life of Cold Mountain had moved on, just as the lives of all connected to the bomber crash had moved on through the years.

By 2004, the Moodys' oldest son, Curtis, was coping with a disability resulting from injuries received while employed by a construction company. He lived in Waynesville with his wife, Loretta, and Loretta's teenage son and daughter, Kenny and Sandy Johnson.

Son Cale, who found the 1944 wire from the bomber when he he was eight years old, had attained a degree in topography from Southern Illinois University, joined the Army, served with the 82nd Airborne in the Gulf War, and was living in Canton with his wife, Brandee, their daughter, Madison Nell Moody, age three; and Brandee's son by her first marriage, John Burnette, age 10.

Cale had been employed for many years by Plemmons Surveyors of Haywood County and had an almost-full-time job as Captain and Company Commander of an Engineering Unit of the Army National Guard. He was sent to Iraq in October, 2005.

Captain Ray Hogue, who had retired after a 24-year Air Force career, was residing in the town of Clyde with his wife, Sue, who had retired as a Registered Nurse at Haywood Regional Hospital.

Their daughter, Susan, was a resident of Chapel Hill, N.C. and was Glaxo Pharmaceutical's Global Sales Manager of medications prescribed for treatment of neurotic and psychological disorders.

Early in his military career, Captain Hogue earned a degree in chemistry at Texas State University, and worked for 14 years as a research chemist in the Air Force.

He was an aircraft maintenance officer, and his duties included investigating plane crashes--just as Major Theodore J. Hieatt had done on Cold Mountain and surrounding areas in the 1940's.

Upon his military retirement, Captain Hogue returned to Haywood County and was employed by Southern Concrete Materials, retiring as Corporate Human Resources Advisor.

It was especially fortuitous that he made the hike to Cold Mountain on that day in May of 2004, because his experience in investigating military plane crashes allowed him to pinpoint the exact spot where the B-25 bomber made impact 58 years earlier.

On a crumbling rock face, the tell-tale sign was a three-foot "ledge" of a deeper crater that nature had filled with dirt and rocks.

Mack Ledbetter agreed that it was in the right place to have been the impact point. And he also agreed with Roy Moody that nature had worked overtime in masking once-familiar scenes on The Mountain.

Souvenir-seekers had worked overtime also. It was doubtful that any plane that crashed in an area like Cold Mountain had drawn such great numbers of people wanting to possess some of the wreckage.

Even the bomber's large fuselage, which had caught the rays of winter's sun for many years after the crash, and had sometimes served as shelter for hikers, hunters, and Boy Scouts, had at some point prior to the late 1970s been dismantled or hammered down somehow and carted off The Mountain by persons unknown.

At the site, Captain Hogue expressed amazement that such a feat had been accomplished.

Small pieces of the bomber could be found here and there around the crash site and on other parts of The Mountain even after the engines had been removed, but there was no trace of anything when the four veterans made their visit in May of 2004.

(And if the engines had stayed in place any longer they probably would have been too skillfully covered by nature to have been found again--especially following torrential rains that caused mud and rock slides and devastating floods spawned by hurricanes Frances and Ivan in Haywood and other western North Carolina counties in September of 2004.)

Before heading back down Cold Mountain, the four men stood at the bomber's impact point wondering if or when they would see it again, or if anyone else would recognize it for what it was when coming years would stretch into decades and current generations would be replaced by new.

By law, no monument could be established at the crash site, and the rock face was too unstable to be engraved with the date of the crash and the names of Major General Paul B. Wurtsmith of Michigan, Lieutenant Colonel Fred L. Trickey Jr. of Wisconsin, Lieutenant Colonel Paul R. Okerbloom of Ohio, Master Sergeant Hosey W. Merritt of Alabama, and Staff Sergeant Hoyt W. Crump of Georgia.

On The Mountain, Roy Moody thought of all the experiences he had had since that 1978 summer day when he was overwhelmed by the 1946 news article about the bomber crash on microfilm. He thought of all the places he had been and the wonderful people he had met, the friendships he had made and renewed, all because of his renewed memory of the crash--a tragedy that in the whole scheme of things may even have saved his life.

He thought of all the times he felt certain there was nothing left to learn or do in relation to the bomber crash. The last time he had been wrong about that was just before he answered his phone two months earlier, and a woman's voice had said, "Mr. Moody, I'm interested in writing a book about the B-25 bomber crash on Cold Mountain."

He would never again say that more could not be learned, or done--but he and the author were both aware that Time and The Mountain would hold some secrets forever.

And on that spring day in 2004, Roy Moody, Captain Ray Hogue, Mack Ledbetter, and Gay Calhoun thought of the young heroes who died on The Mountain. They thought of what they did willingly for America and the world, and for the freedom that allowed them to partake of the blessings of life in the greatest nation on earth.

Then the four veterans left Cold Mountain to its duties that would perhaps remain forever unchanged--harboring frigid howling winds and deep snows in winter; soaking in the laurel-budding warmth of spring; adjusting to heat and horrific storms while preparing its offerings of huckleberries in summer--and remaining respectfully silent on late summer and autumn nights, when katydids fill the air with their lonesome serenades.

On The Mountain, and in human lives, season would always follow season--and as Dr. Hoyt W. Crump II, Roy Moody, and many others would always know in their heart of hearts--*EVERYTHING WOULD HAPPEN FOR A REASON.*

*****

ACKNOWLEDGMENTS

This book would not have been possible without the kind and varied assistance of numerous people in several states.

Special thanks to the staff of the Burton Historical Collection in the Detroit Public Library for photos and information about Major General Paul B. Wurtsmith; to Fred L. Trickey III of New York City for photos and information about Lieutenant Colonel Fred L. Trickey Jr.; to Richard Oakley of Florida for photos and information about Lieutenant Colonel Paul R. Okerbloom; to Jerry Merritt and Esther Payne of Alabama for photos and information about Master Sergeant Hosey W. Merritt; and to Dr. Hoyt W. Crump II of Georgia for photos infomation about Staff Sergeant Hoyt W. Crump.

The following is the author's and Roy Moody's combined list of others in North Carolina to be thanked for helping in a variety of ways--the staff of the Haywood County Public Library, *The Mountaineer* , *Asheville Citizen-Times,* and *News & Observer* newspapers; Gail Moody, O.C. Chambers, Mack and Ethel Ledbetter, Maxine and Junior Sorrells, Audrey Burnette, Paul Erwin.

Louie Reece, Paul and Christine Woody, Mack Warren, Joyce Norris Mease, Roy Norris (deceased), Tommy Burke (deceased), the Jim Burke family, Kenneth Lindsey (deceased), Frank Chambers (deceased), Ned Norris (deceased).

Blanche Norris, Troy Hargrove, Ted Darrell Inman, Verlin Messer, James H. Messer Jr., Elizabeth "E.B." Ivey, Steve Rollins, Maxine Mann Kinsland, Arlen Heatherly, Austin

Thompson, Mrs. Steve Thompson, Lessley D. Griffin, Bill and Wilhelmina Rhodarmer, Kenneth Underwood, Wanda Earley, J.M. Long, Emily Michal Terrell, Reba Frady McCracken, Donald Taylor, Reba Wiggins, John Rhodarmer Jr., C. Max Burnette, Jack Harkins, Sam Henson, Bob Paxton, Robert Cathey, and Joanna Neal Penland, all of Haywood County.

Anne Wells Taylor and Robert Fisher of Asheville; Thomas Lynn Wells of Arden; Eric Huffman and Jean Dodd of Smithfield; Holt Thornton of Wake County, and the author's daughters and son, Leslie Cannon Pennington of Angier, Beth Cannon of Selma, and Jim Cannon of Smithfield.

Roy Moody also thanks Shirley and Frank Wurtsmith (deceased) and family of Detroit; Kent and Marti Steele of Alaska; Larry and LeAnn Fritch and Harold and Madonna Steele of Ohio; all the helpful personnel at Wurtsmith Air Force Base in 1983 and 1989, including Paul Turner, Larry Dawson, Theda Furlonge, Mike Montgomery, and Mike McCann--wherever they may be at the time of this publication.

The author also thanks the following:--in Michigan: Glenn Wurtsmith, Margaret Wilcox, Colonel James B. McLaughlin, director, and volunteers with the Yankee Air Museum at Oscoda; members of the Oscoda VFW Post; staff of Cathy's Hallmark Shop in Oscoda; and Lynn and Denise Hutchinson of Alcona County.

In Wisconsin--the Wisconsin Historical Society, Madison; Madison Public Library; Karen Peterson of Berlin Public Library, Berlin; and Berlin Historical Society.

In Arkansas, Michael Peven, chairman, University of Arkansas (Fayetteville) Art Department; and. in Vermont, Mary Clouser.

In Alabama--Geneva Public Library, Geneva; William Burns, superintendent of Geneva County Schools; Jerry and Kay Merritt of Eufaula; Gail Speigner and Rev. Danny Wiggins of Enterprise and County Line Baptist Church; Esther Payne of Dothan; Acie Taylor, Clyde Justice, and Samuel Quillar of Geneva; and staff of U.S. Army Aviation Museum, Fort Rucker.

Also, Dwight McCarter of Tennessee and the staff of the Military Personnel Records Center, St. Louis, Missouri.

The author also thanks the many people she contacted who were unable to provide information, but were courteous and kind, and expressed interest in the book topic.

She and Roy Moody apologize to those whose names may have been accidentally omitted.

Doris Rollins Cannon

A resident of the Clayton/Smithfield area of Johnston County, N.C., Doris Rollins Cannon maintains close ties to her native Bethel community near Cold Mountain. She is the widow of an Air Force pilot, Captain Lloyd J. Cannon Jr., a native of Canton, N.C., who died of natural causes in 1964. She has one son, two daughters, four grandchildren, two step-grandchildren, and two step-great-grandchildren.

Ms. Cannon was a staff writer and columnist for *The Smithfield Herald* from 1970 to 1990, and was recipient of numerous state press awards. She is the author of *Grabtown Girl: Ava Gardner's North Carolina Childhood and Her Enduring Ties to Home* (published by Down Home Press in 2001); a mini-drama, *Voices on Bethel Cemetery Hill* (presented in her native community in 1997 and 1998); *Echoes from Pascalina,* a 200-year history of the family of Dr. Felix O. Pascalis, a French physician who came to America in 1793 (published by Wayne Hitt in 1995); and *Johnston!,* a two-hour drama based on Johnston County history (performed at Johnston Community College in 1989).

2011 UPDATE

This section is dedicated in memory of Roy Moody's best friend from school days--USAF Captain (Ret.) Riley Ray Hogue of Clyde, N.C.

As noted earlier, there were many links in the chain of events leading the author to contact Roy Moody concerning his knowledge of the bomber crash on Cold Mountain, and this book might never have been written without the link forged when Roy and his old pal, Ray Hogue, ran into each other in Hardee's restaurant in Waynesville in summer of 1983.

During their first conversation in many years, Captain Hogue was surprised to learn that Major General Paul B. Wurtsmith died in the crash on Cold Mountain, and Roy was surprised to learn that an Air Force Base in Michigan was named in Wurtsmith's honor. (Captain Hogue had made inspections at the base during his military career.)

Roy's intense childhood interest in the bomber crash was reignited that day, and he and his wife, Gail, visited Wurtsmith Air Force Base during one of their trips north and continued to garner more crash information.

Captain Hogue's May, 2004 hike to the Cold Mountain crash site   (with Roy, Mack Ledbetter, and Gay Calhoun) was an heroic effort on his part.

His wife, Sue, explained, "On April 18, 1996, Ray suffered a devastating head injury in an auto accident. This resulted in permanent brain damage and a remaining lifetime of seizures, memory loss, and other frustrating deficits. Against many significant odds, he survived brain surgery and was able to live a relatively normal life despite his emotional struggle with his remaining mental deficits."

On April 18, 2006, Captain Hogue passed away following a massive heart attack, which was determined to be the end result of his car accident exactly 10 years earlier.

His time spent on Cold Mountain on that spring day in 2004 was uplifting in many ways, not the least of which was his ability to recall his experiences inspecting plane crashes during his military service, and thereby being able to point out the likely spot that the B-25 bomber made its fateful impact on The Mountain.

The Cold Mountain venture was a special victory for Captain Hogue, and also for his boyhood buddy and the many others who knew and loved this remarkable man.

*****

A number of residents of Haywood County, N.C. whose lives were impacted by the bomber crash are still living, and many died long before this book was first published in 2005. Some had larger parts in the story than others, but all played a vital role in the crash history. Those who have passed on since 2005 are as follows:

Mack Ledbetter, who led the May, 2004 Cold Mountain hike with Hogue, Moody, and Calhoun, climbed to the crest of Heaven's highest mountain on November 14, 2007. He was 75-years-old when he came to the end of a long and valiant struggle against cancer.

Ethel, his wife of 54 years, followed in June of 2008.

It is doubtful that any man will ever know Cold Mountain as well as Mack, who as a teenager helped military officials recover bodies of the five heroes who died in the B-25 crash, and in his retirement years completed around 75 hikes to the crash site.

Mack loved all the mountains that were part and parcel of his life in western North Carolina's beautiful Pigeon River Valley, and that love will long be remembered and cherished by his descendants and many friends.

*****

(In spring of 2011, Gay Calhoun of Canton, who made the May 2004 climb to the bomber crash site, was continuing to hike wherever and whenever possible. "I do it any time I can get somebody to go with me," said the youthful 87-year-old, and he told Roy Moody, "If I make it to 90, I want you to hike up Cold Mountain with me again."

A World War II Army Air Force veteran, Gay was a gunner and bombardier on B-25s, B-24s, and B-26s.)

*****

Robert Wayne "Monk" Fisher, who as a teenager in 1946 helped his pals Bill Rhodarmer and Stuart Smathers roll one of the B-25 wheels off Cold Mountain, died of heart failure on August 7, 2009. He was 77 years-old.

Through the years, the tire rim was used as a flower planter in the Rhodarmer yard in Canton, N.C.

Louie Reece, who told Roy Moody how to get to the bomber crash site, and after Roy's failed first attempt drew him a precise map, died of colon cancer at age 76 on January 24, 2007.

Lawrence "Toad" Birchfield, who grew up at the foot of Cold Mountain, and guided many hikers to the crash scene, including "Ish" Lawrence's Boy Scout Troop from Canton, died of heart failure on March 1, 2009. He was 81.

Jack Lyerly, one of the members of the Boy Scout Troop, died at age 74 of COPD (Chronic Obstructive Pulmonary Disease) on August 28, 2006.

The Scouts brought one of the blades from the bomber's propeller off the mountain, and it was displayed in the Canton Museum.

(The only living member of the Scout Troop at the time of this writing was 78-year-old Carroll "Gene" Devlin of Canton, who served in the Air Force during the Korean War and retired from Champion International with 38 years of service.)

Joe Sales, who as a seventh-grader was forced to stay home from school because he had eaten too many of the luscious grapes that had ripened in Pigeon River Valley, died following a long battle with Parkinson's disease on November 10, 2010. While in the family's "outhouse," he heard the awful roar of the bomber a few seconds before it hit Cold Mountain. Joe was 77 at the time of his death.

Jack Harkins, a member of the men's "Liars Club," that in 2011 still met for breakfast at Hardee's restaurant in Canton, died of sudden heart failure at age 77 on May 19, 2010.

(It was a friendly Liars Club argument about the date of the bomber crash that led the author to make contact with Roy Moody and launch the book project.)

*****

Roy Moody will also never forget his long-time friend Hilliard Jones of Waynesville, who persuaded him to attend his first NACAR Grand National Race (now known as Sprint Cup) at the old Asheville-Weaverville Speedway on March 4, 1962.

After that exciting event, Roy became a devoted race fan, and he and his wife and sons began traveling to races near and far and on vacations to places they'd never seen, including Wurtsmith Air Force Base.

A victim of multiple myloma, Hilliard Jones died on August 27, 1998 at age 58.

*****

DESCENDANTS OF THE HEROES

Major General Paul B. Wurtsmith had no direct descendants, and Sgt. Hosey W. Merritt's closest kin of the next generation was his nephew, Jerry Merritt. The three little boys made fatherless by the bomber crash were: Hoyt W. Crump II, son of Sgt. Hoyt W. Crump and wife Margaret; Fred L. Trickey III, son of Lt. Col. Fred L. Trickey Jr., and wife Peggy: and Paul Richard "Dickie" Okerbloom Jr., son of Lt. Col. Paul Richard "Pete" Okerbloom and wife Marie.

Fred L. Trickey III, a noted computer and "information security" expert living and working in New York City, died following heart problems and an extended illness on May 5, 2010. He was 65-years-old.

After Fred's father died on Cold Mountain and his mother married Air Force Major James Bratton Lampley, Fred grew up in Hendersonville, N.C., where he was adopted into the Lampley family and was as much a part of it as those born with the name.

For a time in his early years, he was known as Fred Lampley, but later he and his mother thought it best that he return to the Trickey name as a tribute to the very small Trickey family and the father he never knew. (His mother was widowed again when Major Lampley died of cancer at age 35 in 1954.)

Fred Trickey III was survived by his brother, famed network sportscaster Jim Lampley of Del Mar, California, and three nieces and a nephew.

He was proud of all his brother's children, and was especially happy to have niece Brooke Lampley as a fellow New Yorker. Brooke, age 31, was a 2002 summa cum laude graduate of Harvard University. She was a dealer of Modern and Impressionist art, and the first female vice president in the New York office of Christie's Fine Art Auction House. She was administrator of the May, 2010 auction that produced a "realized amount" of over $106 million for a Picasso painting. It was a world record for the artist and also a world record for a work of art sold at auction.

Niece Victoria Lampley, 24, was a graduate of Bard College in upstate New York. She was director of public relations for the Brompton nightclub and restaurant chain in London, England.

Niece Andrea Walker, 23, (Jim's stepdaughter) was involved in real estate on the north shore of Oahu, Hawaii, and nephew Aaron James Lampley, 20, was a student majoring in English Literature at Santa Monica College in California.

Jim Lampley and his wife, TV anchor Bree Walker, were divorced, on good terms, in 2000 and he had remained single since that time.

In Hendersonville, Fred Trickey III was survived by his uncle and aunt, Dr. William A. Lampley, a retired surgeon, and wife Mary Ann; and cousins, as follows: William A. "Bill" Lampley Jr., a professional actor, musician, playwright, and sometime corporate analyst in the entertainment industry; John Lampley, who was employed by First Presbyterian Church of Hendersonville and had his own Christian counseling service; and Margie Lampley Capell, who for many years played French Horn with the Greenville (S.C.) Symphony and the Flathills Brass Quartet. She became a special education teacher at Hendersonville High School and was a popular soprano vocalist and music coach.

Fred's surviving cousins in Norfolk, VA were Robert Hoyt "Pete" Lampley Jr., an inhalation therapist; and Gregory "Reed" Lampley, a successful office supply merchant and philanthropic volunteer ombudsman for the elderly.

In 2011, Jim Lampley was covering boxing on television's Home Box Office (HB0) and headed his own production company, Atticus Entertainment.

He said his brother Fred was "the most authentic person" he had ever known, and also one of the most courageous.

As noted in the Lt. Col. Fred L. Trickey Jr. chapter, the boys' mother, Peggy Trickey Lampley, was an extraordinary woman whose second son by Lt. Col. Trickey was born dead several months after the bomber crash. She was twice-widowed before she was 35-years-old, and she moved forward and raised her two sons with unflinching self-assurance, determination and courage.

Those traits, and the heroic aspects of Fred's and Jim's World War II pilot fathers, were passed on to the boys.

Fred III summoned unusual courage early in life.

Jim Lampley said his brother "came out of the closet" when he was in his mid-teens, a time when such a thing was very rare.

Like his mother, Fred faced the challenges and facts of his life head-on, and never pretended to be anything other than the person he was.

Jim said Fred loved life in New York City. A brilliant and talented man, who once considered an acting career, he meshed well with the city that provided so many opportunities for cultural enrichment.

When the author was making an extensive search for surviving kin of the men who died on Cold Mountain, she had almost given up hope of finding Fred Trickey III. But around 2 a.m. one morning, she awoke suddenly with an urge to turn on her computer. It was as if "something" had nudged her and instructed her to do that. Still half asleep, she logged onto the Internet, and "Googled" the name Fred L. Trickey III, as she had done many times before.

Instantly, a page opened, and there was an announcement that the object of her search would be speaking at a conference on information security.

Early the next morning, Fred answered the phone in his New York apartment, and was surprised and pleased to learn that a book was being written about his father and the other men who died on Cold Mountain.

He said that the day before the author's phone call, he had been looking through his special box marked "DAD" for the first time in ages. The box contained photos of Lt. Col. Trickey, what was left of his uniform at the crash site on Cold Mountain, and other treasured items passed down by Fred's mother.

And so the final link of the bomber crash story was completed.

In September of 2010, the month that coincidentally marked the 64th anniversary of Lt. Col. Trickey's death, Jim Lampley went to New York City for a memorial service honoring his brother.

And he sprinkled his ashes in a park close to his home near the Hudson River, in Central Park's Strawberry Fields, and some of Fred's other favorite sites in the city he loved so well.

It was a tribute that would have pleased Lt. Col. Fred L. Trickey Jr., Major James B. Lampley, Peggy Trickey Lampley--and the man who lived life with honesty and integrity to the end.

*****

Richard "Dick" (Okerbloom) Oakley of Boca Raton, Florida, passed away on May 27, 2010, only 22 days following the death of Fred Trickey III.

The son of Lt. Col. Paul Richard "Pete" Okerbloom, Dick's name was changed to the similar-sounding Oakley after being adopted at age eight by his step-father, Bert Tuttle Oakley.

At age 68, Dick Oakley passed away following a six-month battle with lung cancer. (His mother died of lung cancer in 1984 at age 66.)

A true family man who delighted in his children and grandchildren, Dick lived long enough to enjoy his youngest granddaughter, Payton, daughter of his son

Kurt Richard Oakley and second wife Amy (see family photo on page 88). Payton was three-years-old at the time of her grandfather's death.

At the time of this writing, the family was looking forward to the birth of Kurt and Amy's second child, a boy to be named Logan Richard Oakley.

The baby will be the third in Lt. Col. Paul Richard Okerbloom's direct ancestral line to bear his middle name.

Dick Oakley's widow, Joyce, still lived in Boca Raton and kept happily busy "baby-sitting" Payton, and said she would do the same for baby Logan.

Dick's other beloved grandchildren were Taylor Oakley, Kurt's daughter by a previous marriage; who was 15 in 2011; and Tate and Jake Johnson, daughter and son of Megan Oakley Johnson and husband Ryan, who were 13 and 11, respectively.

In 2011, Dick and Joyce's sons Kurt and Evan, and daughter Megan continued to reside and work in the Boca Raton area, and son Bret lived and worked in Raleigh, N.C.

Joyce said her husband Dick was like Peter Pan, the high-flying fictional lad who never aged, and she often referred to him as her fifth child. "He was just one of the kids," she said--a fun-loving prankster who never allowed any place or situation to become boring.

A talented graphic artist, he was also a kid when at work with the powerful IBM Corporation. All male employees were expected to wear suits and ties, and one day Dick cut his tie in half, and announced, "This is what happens when I get my tie caught in the paper cutter!"

On another occasion, he fell to the floor at IBM and played dead.

The Oakley family lived on the beach and often chartered a sailboat and traveled to places like the Virgin Islands. They did all the sailing themselves, and daughter Megan fondly recalls her father serving as a very funny instructor for a family course he titled "Rope-Throwing 101."

Joyce recalled, "Dick was the sailboat Captain and I was the Mate. We did things like swim with the turtles, and there were times when we ran aground or had to dive in and retrieve things that had fallen overboard. Dick hid 'treasures' on the islands and made maps to help the children find them. He told them the maps had been drawn by pirates, and of course the treasures had been hidden by those dreadful villains of long ago.

"Everything we did was wonderful," Joyce recalled.

Nancy Baer Morris of Belmar, N.J. was Dick's cousin on his mother's side of the   family. Her father, Donald Baer, was Marie Baer Okerbloom Oakley's brother.

Recalling years of her childhood, Nancy said Cousin Dick visited the Baer family home in New Jersey for about a week during the summers of his teen years.

He was older than Nancy and her two sisters and two brothers, and she said he treated them with kindness and a great deal of patience. During one summer visit, he helped her brothers Don and Tom build a wood and canvas canoe in their back yard.

Nancy also recalled that her brothers used a duffle bag with the name "Okerbloom" printed on it during their years in Boy Scouts. It obviously came from the trunk in the Baer home, which contained the mementos of Lt. Col. Okerbloom's too-brief life.

When Nancy's father, Donald Baer, died in 1982, her brother, TSgt. Don Baer, was serving in the Air Force in England and flew home for the funeral.

Marie Baer Okerbloom Oakley, then age 64, and Dick Oakley, who was in his late 30s, were present for Donald's funeral. Afterward, Marie commented that she was startled when her nephew emerged from a taxi wearing his Air Force uniform. She said it reminded her of the September day in 1946, when military personnel came tto break the awful news that her husband had died in the B-25 crash.

Thirty-six years had passed since Lt. Col. Okerbloom's death on Cold Mountain, but for his widow, in that moment at her brother's funeral, the passing of time was meaningless. "I worried about him all through World War II," Marie said, "and for him to be killed in peacetime was just rotten."

For Dick Oakley, seeing his cousin in uniform brought a more comforting flashback to his childhood. It reminded him of when his Uncle Donald Baer, who also served during World War II, came home from Europe wearing his Army Air Force uniform a few days before Christmas of 1946. It was the first Christmas following the tragedy on Cold Mountain, and Donald Baer did all he could to help ease the pain for his widowed sister and fatherless nephew.

Nancy Baer Morris said she was surprised to learn of her cousin Dick Oakley's death, because when she talked to him on the phone he was always upbeat and never complained about a thing. He was an "eternal optimist."

Dick's half-brother, Scott Oakley, retired after 28 years with the City of Phoenix, Arizona, and in 2011 he and his wife, Linda Masucci, were enjoying a relaxed life in North Phoenix.

Dick was 11 years older than Scott, who recalled, "He was my idol for many years, and our relationship grew from that to being best friends with brotherly love. I've never had another relationship as special as that in my life. Dick never got mad at me, even when I pressed the garage door remote control too soon and it came down on the convertible top of his brand new 1967 Austin Healy as we were backing out of the garage. It even left a tiny hole in the canvas."

Scott said the incident later made him realize his brother "was simply a gentle soul who took everything in stride."

As Scott grew older, he began noticing that his big brother possessed some things that other members of the family did not. "He was talented in ways that others were not," Scott said. "And he had facial features unlike other family members. Strangely, things that stood out most to me were his fingers. They were very long and slender."

Dick Oakley had the hands of an artist. (See page

79 about Dick's biological uncle, Charles L. Okerbloom Jr., a renowned professional artist and art professor at the University of Arkansas.)

Finally, when he was around 15-years-old in the late 1960s, Scott came right out at the dinner table one night and asked his parents why his brother was so different from the rest of the family. His mother gently put down her fork and said, "Well, Scott, we knew this day would come." She went on to explain that Dick's biological father was an outstanding Army Air Force officer who died in a B-25 bomber crash in 1946. And Scott's father, Bert Oakley, added, "Yes, Scott, and we have something else to tell you too."

Still reeling from the first revelation about his brother Dick, young Scott thought, "My God! Can it be that I'm not who I think I am?!"

Then his father told him he had another son, Robert, through his first marriage. And therefore Robert was Scott's half-brother also.

"I knew Robert, but no one had ever told me exactly who he was," Scott said. "It was all somewhat of a shock."

But the teenager absorbed the astonishing information quickly, and then thought, "Well, but this doesn't change anything between me and Dick, does it?"

Of course it did not, and just like Fred L. Trickey III and his half-brother, Jim Lampley, the "half" was never even a small part of their lives. As far as they were concerned, they were true and full brothers forever.

In April of 2011, Dick Oakley's son, Kurt, traveled to Melbourne, Florida on business. It was where Marie and Bert Oakley lived out their days, and where they were laid to rest.

Some of Dick's ashes were placed there also. The rest were to be sprinkled along with his wife's following her passing.

Kurt recalled, "The beaches at Melbourne are where my father taught me to surf, on a surfboard that we constructed together one summer in my youth.

"In a nearby coastal bay is where he took me clamming, in the mud flats. And nearby is Cape Canaveral, where the space shuttle Challenger was launched and destroyed on a fateful day in 1986. My father and I watched the disaster together on live TV.

"None of this really hit me until I was sitting in a restaurant in Melbourne, which had a surfboard displayed on the wall. I noticed the tail of the board was shaped in a certain angle-wedged sort of way--the same shape used on our homemade board.

"This triggered the memory of my father and me building the board, learning to surf in the waters at Melbourne, the clamming, and the shuttle disaster--all random memories triggered from glancing at the back end of a surfboard.

"This kind of thing happens for me at other surprising times also. Making a quick trip to a home improvement store on a usual busy weekend, and seeing a certain tool on the rack, reminds me of some other tool my father taught me to use. And that in turn reminds me of a piece of furniture I have in my house that he helped me build, and that reminds me of working together on radio-controlled airplanes, which we always managed to crash--so we would have to go together to the home improvement store to get materials to re-build it.

"In just about everything I do, and in everything I am, my father is somehow there with me--and I hope it stays that way."

In remembering the father that Dick Oakley never knew, a friend of Lt. Col. Paul Richard "Pete" Okerbloom wrote, in part, in 1946: "He was all that was worthwhile and commendable. He was natural, human, enjoyed life deeply, and transmitted some of that spirit to all he touched."

And that certainly included the little boy he lovingly called "Dickie."

*****

Dr. Hoyt W. Crump II of Franklin Springs, Georgia retired from his family medical practice on December 31, 2010. He had been providing healing and comfort to patients for 38 ½ years.

The first five years were with a group of doctors who served several hospital emergency rooms in Atlanta, and the remaining years were with Royston Medical Associates of Royston, Georgia, near his home.

Born on June 10, 1946, Dr. Crump was only three months and threedays old when his father, Sgt. Hoyt

W. Crump of Hart County, Georgia, died at age 27 in the B-25 crash on Cold Mountain.

Young Hoyt was raised by his mother, Margaret, who made sure that he became an important part of his father's large family in Georgia. His devoted step-father was Jeff Askew, who also served in World War II.

Shortly after Thanksgiving of 2009, Dr. Crump was faced with a devastating family medical situation he could do nothing about, nor could specialists in the ear, nose, and throat medical field.

Roy Crump, the 35-year-old son of Dr. Crump and his wife Lee, was suddenly struck by a viral infection that left him disabled.

The infection, which settled in his middle ear, destroyed the hearing in his left ear and many noises entering his right ear sounded like gunshots or the pounding of kettle drums, a condition known as "tinnitus."

Roy's equilibrium was also adversely affected, a condition known as "labyrinthitis," and it became necessary for him to walk with a cane. And he could no longer drive a car.

He moved to Norcross, Georgia from the Silicon Valley area of California, where he was involved in an exciting career in the animation and printing technology.

In the sixth grade, Roy learned to operate a computer in the Gifted Students Program at Royston Elementary School. He had a skill which was an outgrowth of his natural artistic talent.

He received a BA degree in art, with a minor in drama, from Piedmont College at Demorest, Georgia, and later studied computer animation for two years in California.

An expert with Hewlett-Packard's Indigo systems, which imprint photos and other artwork on coffee mugs, plates, and other objects, he traveled extensively as a trouble-shooter in that field.

As vicious as Roy's viral infection proved to be, it was unable to destroy his spirit, his talent, or his interest in computers. He was unable to have gainful employment, but worked hard toward regaining his computer skills after moving to Norcross.

His parents visited him often and assisted in any way possible, and he was able to have a limited social life with friends who lived nearby and assisted him whenever needed.

"He has kept a good attitude," his mother said, "and has tried not to dwell on his problem."

She said that, although nerve damage is close to impossible to remedy, the family will not give up hope that medical science will come up with a way to help her son in the future.

The Crumps' daughter, Dessie, age 33 in 2011, was named for her great-grandmother, the late Dessie Ayers Crump of Hart County, Georgia.

In her second year of junior college, she married Adam Mazhar, and later became a dedicated mother of two.

Dessie is a stay-at-home Mom and "the ultimate Soccer Mom," who spends a great deal of time taking

236

her son, Noah Hoyt, age 12 in 2011; and Alyssa Lee, 7 ½, to their many activities. (Noah Hoyt Mazhar is the third male in Sgt. Crump's line of direct descendants to have Hoyt as a first or middle name. Alyssa Lee Mazhar is the third in the female line of descendants to carry the name Lee.

Adam Mazhar earned a BS degree in business administration from Georgia State University at Atlanta and completed a two-year course in computer science at Gwinnett Technical College in Lawrenceville, Georgia.

He was a civilian employee at Maxwell Air Force Base in Alabama for two years and another two years at Warner Robins Air Force Base in Georgia. Then he was transferred to Saudi Arabia, where the family lived until sand storms in the desert proved detrimental to little Alyssa's health. Dessie and the children returned to Georgia and lived with Dr. and Mrs. Crump for a year prior to her husband's return to the States.

By 2011, Adam Mazhar had worked for over three years at the large Federal facility at Clarksburg, West Virginia.

Dr. and Mrs. Crump's youngest son, Charles Hoyt "Charlie," was 27 years old in 2011 and making plans to marry Lauren Redman of Gainesville, Georgia, in November.

He had his own web site design company and was manager of a business which markets NASCAR memorabilia worldwide through the Internet.

His fiancé earned a degree in accounting, was

working on a master's degree, and was a financial officer with a firm in Gainesville.

In 2011, Laura Righton, age 88, Lee Crump's mother, had been a beloved and welcome member of the Crump household for several years. She was a victim of Alzheimer's disease.

Lee said that her mother and father met when both were serving in the Marine Corps in the final years of World War II. Her mother was a Pfc. and her father was a 1st Lt. and therefore any social contact between the two was forbidden. But love has a way of creating a safe path, and they were married in 1946.

Dr. Crump's step-father   remained unattached following the death of Margaret Crump Askew in 1994.

At age 87, Jeff Askew was in good health and often seen driving his Jaguar around Atlanta. He gets together with the Crump family several times each year.

Peggy Ann Askew Smith of Jackson, Georgia, Dr. Crump's half-sister, was continuing her career in nursing in 2011. Ken and Jennifer Rivers, her son and daughter by her first marriage, were insurance agents in Locust Grove, Georgia.

Margaret Crump Askew was a creative seamstress, and Dr. Crump said the artistic side of his family came from her and from his grandmother, Dessie Crump, who loved flowers and always had a spectacular garden.

He stays in contact with his aunt, Jan Crump Burgess, who has won many awards for her exquisite flowers. He also stays in touch with his uncle, Alton Crump, who was 87 years old in 2011.

Not at all left out of the family's artistic legacy, Dr. Crump's spare time was often filled with digging holes for something beautiful to be planted on his property. And he earlier designed the interior of his and Lee's house.

Another of his past-time pleasures was attending NASCAR races. His favorite driver was Tony Stewart, who had a quick temper and often kept things stirred up on the track and off, but also showed his kind and generous nature by standing up for older drivers, such as James Hylton, who was still racing at age 76; and Morgan Shepherd, nearing age 70, who Stewart assisted by providing tires for his race car.

Lee Crump, who worked as a Registered Nurse and spent a number of years assisting young mothers who wanted to breast-feed their babies, made another mark in the world after an accident injury led to her early retirement in 1976.

She became a rescuer of animals, mostly dogs, and through her work with the Hart County Humane Society, she has "foster trained" around 20 dogs per year and prepared them for adoption in loving homes. The Crumps also had an active horse farm for 20 years.

In January of 2008, Lee Crump became an elder in Hartwell Presbyterian Church, and Dr. Crump did the same in January of 2011.

When he retired from his medical practice, he found that it wasn't easy to let go.

Those who began work at Royston Medical Associates often remained in their posts for 40 or 50 years, creating a special kind of family, and one to be greatly missed.

Dr. Crump also missed his patients and the blessing of being able to help them through some of the small or severe storms of life.

He could not give that up entirely, so in mid-2011 he began volunteering his services part-time at charity clinics in Athens and Toccoa, Georgia.

The 27-year-old Army Air Force Sergeant, who didn't make it home to his wife and child on September 13, 1946, would certainly have been proud of the man his baby boy became.

Jerry Merritt. who was five-years-old when his uncle, Sergeant Hosey W. Merritt, died in the Cold Mountain bomber crash, was old enough to have some lasting memories of the high-spirited, talented, charming and witty Alabama farm boy who died at age 28.

Sgt. Merritt was divorced and had no children at the time of his death, but he loved children and doted on young Jerry and nieces Mary Ellen and Janice Marie.

Jerry idolized his Uncle, and not only inherited his artistic talent, but carried it into a career in advertising and to becoming a professional painter of historic buildings and other scenes in his retirement years.

In 2011, Jerry and wife Kay, also an artist, still lived in Eufala, Alabama, and continued participating in art exhibits in that area. Kay's floral paintings were especially popular.

For the Merritt family, 2006-2009 were years of heart-breaking losses and serious health problems. Kay's mother, Carrie Harvey, died in May of 2006. She had spent the last year of her life with Jerry and Kay.

On December 29, 2006, Kay's son, Darren Hallman, died unexpectedly of heart failure. He was 44 years old.

Jerry's mother, Esther Payne of Dothan, Alabama, died in January of 2007, and that same week Kay Merritt almost died following open-heart surgery.

In August of 2009, Jerry and a friend were injured when a dump truck rear-ended their stopped vehicle. One of Jerry's injuries was a torn rotator cuff, which could not be repaired through surgery and therefore continued to give him pain, and he had several operations to repair two holes in each retina of both eyes.

In May, 2011, Jerry's brother-in-law, Bob Heinemann, passed away.

The good news was that other family members were doing well, including Jerry's daughter, Jennifer and son-in-law, Dr. Todd Hansen of Gastonia, N.C. and their children: Stewart, age 17; Abbie, 14, and Sara, 8.

Kay Merritt's two daughters, son, and seven grandchildren were well also.

A mystery unsolved by 2011 involved a situation encountered by Jerry and Kay in January of 2010, when they made a trip to County Line Baptist Church Cemetery, near Enterprise, Alabama, to check on the

Merritt family plot.

In 1946, Sgt. Merritt's grief-stricken father, Charlie, decided to include all the names of the men who died on Cold Mountain on the large flat stone over his beloved son's grave. (See page 104)

As years went by, forces of nature took a toll on the memorial for the five heroes. Jerry and Kay did what they could too keep it and the other Merritt tombstones free of unwelcome stains, and helping finance the upkeep of the plot were Jerry's mother, sisters Mary Ellen Heinemann and Janice Marie Bush; and his step-brother, Greg Jordan. Kay's children also assisted with the project.

Jerry was told that some stains were "embedded" in Sgt. Merritt's stone and could not be removed.

In addition to the large memorial for Sgt. Merritt and the other four heroes, the plot included a stone on the grave of Jerry's daughter by his first marriage. Melanie Merritt was only one-year- old when she died on January 3, 1966 of what was determined to be an unsuspected liver malfunction which she had had from birth. His second daughter, Jennifer, was born with the same problem, but medication was able to keep it under control.

Laid to rest near little Melanie was Charlie Merritt, who lived a fruitful 97 years, and Sgt. Merritt's mother, Ada, who died at age 85 in 1965. On one stone was the name of Charlie's second wife, called "Myrtie," but her body was buried in a place closer to her family members.

The Merritt plot was a little hard to spot right

away, since it was located amid so many gravestones in County Line Cemetery--but not when Jerry and Kay arrived there in January of 2010.

As the cemetery came into view, Kay was astonished by what she saw, and exclaimed, "Jerry! Look!"

The stones in the Merritt plot were gleaming like snow in bright winter sun.

And the couple was even more amazed when they reached the plot on foot. All the stones looked as new as the day they were placed in that serene country setting. "And they seemed to be sprinkled with diamonds," Kay said.

Little angels and other figures on Melanie's gravestone were found beside her grave, as if waiting to be put back in place by her father.

Who had done the remarkable cleaning of the stones? Why had Jerry and Kay not been informed?

From the looks of the stones and his own experience, Jerry determined that such a project would have required special equipment taken to the grave sites.

There would have been a powerful and noisy compressor. Surely someone at County Line Baptist Church would know something about it. But the pastor and church secretary said they knew nothing. No one had asked permission to take stone-cleaning equipment into the cemetery; and no person or persons had been seen, and no noise had been heard by people at the church or others living in the area.

Family members and friends said they knew

nothing about the project, so Jerry made calls to the businesses in that area of Alabama that might have been hired for the job. Still no result. Veterans' organizations and groups like the Masons also knew nothing, and so the wonder continued.

The mystery of the sparkling white stone engraved with the image of the American Flag and names of Sgt. Hosey W. Merritt, Maj. Gen. Paul B. Wurtsmith, Lt. Col. Fred L. Trickey Jr., Lt. Col. Paul R. Okerbloom, and Sgt. Hoyt W. Crump may come to a simple solution in time, or it may remain as years drift on.

"I think the stones were cleaned by angels from Heaven," Kay Merritt said.

If not, they were certainly cleaned by angels on earth.

*****

THE STEELES OF ALASKA

Captain Kent Steele, who headed the huge project of lifting the bomber engines off Cold Mountain and taking them to Wurtsmith Air Force Base in Michigan in 1989, was later stationed at Elmendorf Air Base and Fort Richardson Army Base in Alaska. He retired from the Air Force in 1995, and chose to make Alaska his home.

He and his family settled at Delta Junction, where Captain Steele was a P.A. (Physician's Assistant) serving residents of fishing villages in that area.

He built a house there and purchased 2,000 acres of farm and mountain land. He grew hay on several hundred acres, and tried new varieties every year. He also experimented with new varieties of apple trees and with wheat.

The Steeles had chickens to provide eggs, and sheep which provided lambs to sell and wool for Marti to spin, knit, and weave. The couple and daughter Meghan also had horses and ponies, and sold their offspring.

They grew a large garden of potatoes and maintained a greenhouse for tomatoes, peppers, and cucumbers. Each season, the children helped gather wild raspberries, which were used for making jam.

In 2011, Captain Steele was working on Alaska's North Shore as a P.A. serving oil-drilling companies.

He and Marti were parents of 12 children (six boys and six girls) and four grandchildren, as follows:

Matt Steele, age 32, lived in Anchorage, AK, where

he was manager of a new car dealership. He and his wife, Stephanie, had a daughter, Leila, age one.

Eric Steele, 30, of California, was single and had a seven-year-old son, also named Eric. He worked for a company that sold motorized ride-on coolers (light-weight battery powered scooters with front placed drink coolers, popular for use at sporting events, picnics, and the like.).

Meghan Steele Orona, 28, and husband Doug lived at Delta Junction. She received a degree in Psychology from the University of Nebraska and was a coordinator for Deltana Community Human Services. She and her husband had a three-year-old daughter, Isabel, and 18-month-old son, Connor.

Kelly Steele Slechta, 26, earned a degree in Criminal Justice from the University of Alaska and was employed in the State Attorney's Office in Fairbanks. Her husband, Tyler, was in the Air Force.

Kevin Steele, 21, was taking correspondence college courses while living in Anchorage with his brother Matt and family. He served as care-giver for his niece Leila while her parents worked.

Seven children still lived at home in 2011, and were home-schooled by the extraordinary mother Marti. They were: Anne Steele, 18, a native of China; Sean Steele, 17, and Ryan Steele, 14; Jade Steele, 12, a native of China; Katie Steele, 10, and Aiden Steele, 9, both natives of Vietnam; and Erin Steele, 6, a native of Hong Kong.

Amid the swirl of a very full and unusual life, Captain Steele wrote and published two books--a science fiction work titled   Morning Star Rising, and a juvenile fiction titled Stacey's Quest, both available on the Internet through Amazon.com.

Those who know Kent and Marti realize that a grand topic for another book would be the fantastic Steele family itself.

*****

BONDS FROM THE BOMBER CRASH

No one has been more caught up in the history and legacy of the B-25 bomber crash on Cold Mountain than Roy Moody, who as a nine-year-old living near The Mountain spent many days desperately trying to figure out a way he could get to the crash site without being bitten by a poisonous snake or eaten by a panther. He was too deep into his thoughts of the crash site, and maybe being able to save a life, to even consider what punishment he might get from his parents for running away from home.

His childhood obsession with the crash was laid to rest as the turbulent autumn of 1946 yielded to the exciting prospects of Christmas. But enough remained stored inside his soul to awaken again when he was a married man with two small sons.

The boy of 1946 could never have guessed where the crash would lead him in years to come--or the bonds that would be formed because of it.

When the author called Roy and discussed writing a book, the two had never seen or even heard of each other, and they did not meet face-to-face until the day before the book-signing at Frank's Grocery on Cruso Road in Haywood County on September 16, 2005.

Since that time, the Moody and Cannon families have formed a friendship strong enough to last a lifetime.

And that was only the beginning of Roy's additional bonds stemming from the bomber crash.

On April 12, 2008, Roy and his wife Gail traveled to

Enterprise, Alabama and spent the night in a motel. The next morning, they drove the five miles to County Line Baptist Church Cemetery, and paid their respects at the grave of Sgt. Hosey W. Merritt and others in the Merritt family. Roy said that standing beside the large flat stone engraved with all the names of those who died on Cold Mountain brought depth of emotion that is hard to describe.

They arrived in Eufaula, Alabama on the evening of April 15, checked into a motel. They called Jerry Merritt and told him they had arrived and would get a good night's rest. Jerry said he and his wife Kay would meet them there in the morning.

When the sun came up the next day, Roy said he felt almost numb from the anticipation of meeting Sgt. Merritt's nephew. And he also felt queasy, thanks to a too-greasy meal in a fast food restaurant the night before.

When a tall man appeared at the motel room, the first thing he said was, "My gosh, Roy, you've got a pretty wife! Us ugly old boys always get the pretty girls."

With that ice-breaking opening by Jerry Merritt, everything became as easy as if the two couples had known each other for years. And Roy's stomach got back to normal, thanks to a pack of Rolaids. (Roy had asked Jerry to bring him one during their morning phone conversation.)

However, another numbing moment came in the Merritt's living room, when Jerry handed Roy one of Sgt. Merritt's photo albums, with pictures beginning in the 1930s. In that era, albums had sturdy covers and long sheets of black paper, on which photos could be glued or attached by little black adhesive corner-covers. In white ink, young Hosey Merritt had written something under each picture.

Roy told the Merritts, "I can't believe I'm holding this in my hands. I can't even believe I'm here!" Again, the feeling was something he could not put into words.

Several hours were spent looking through the albums and other materials, which brought the guests much closer to Sgt. Merritt's too-brief life and gave them a deeper appreciation of his service during World War II.

On the way to their house, the Merritts had given the Moody's a tour of the picturesque little town of Eufaula, part of which was used in the filming of "Sweet Home, Alabama," a 2002 movie starring Reese Witherspoon as Melanie Carmichael, a successful New York fashion designer returning to her hometown of "Greenville," Alabama to be married. Eufaula's majestic antebellum homes were featured in the movie's opening scenes.

Jerry told the story about a long-time resident of Eufaula who had been out of town for several days and knew nothing about plans for shooting movie scenes. By the time he returned, the film's crew had replaced the Eufaula sign with one naming the town Greenville.

The man said that when he reached what looked like Eufaula, but was a town called Greenville, he thought he was losing his mind.

Jerry Merritt presented Roy and Gail a painting he had done of the famous boll weevil statue in Enterprise. Earlier, the author was sent a gift of Kay's painting of the statue.

They enjoyed a barbecue meal at the White Oak Mart near the Merritt home, and Roy's stomach behaved beautifully.

It had been a wonderful visit.

On April 16, 2010, the couple drove to Georgia, where they spent the night in a motel at the small town of Royston. They drove around town and located the clinic where Dr. Hoyt W. Crump worked for over three decades.

The next day, April 17, was a Sunday, and Roy again experienced the strange emotional feeling akin to numbness. It swept over him just before, and when, Dr. Hoyt W. Crump II, son of the young Sergeant who died on Cold Mountain, walked into the living room of his home at Franklin Springs and warmly greeted the guests from North Carolina. The doctor's wife, Lee, also made them feel very welcome.

The Crumps were usually in church on Sunday, but they skipped that day in order to spend as much time as possible with the man who knew so much about the bomber crash.

After lunch in a cafeteria, the Crumps drove the Moodys through a placid expanse of the Hart County countryside, which had once been the farm where Sgt. Crump grew up. Before them lay the same fields where the father Dr. Crump never knew spent so many long days of his youth picking cotton in the unrelenting heat of summer.

There was nothing left of the old farmhouse. But there was a double row of trees regaled in the welcoming green of another springtime in Georgia, and they led to the spot where the house once stood.

After Sgt. Crump and his parents had passed on, the trees were planted by Dr. Crump's Uncle Alton Crump, who purchased the property.

The tour included a ride by Hartwell Presbyterian Church, where Dr. and Mrs. Crump served as elders, and Reed Creek Baptist Church, where Sgt. Crump's mother, Dessie, was a devout member. They also drove by an old cemetery where the original Reed Creek Church once stood.

Back at home, Dr. Crump and Roy talked about their avid interest in NASCAR, and Roy later mailed his host a news article about Jimmy Crawford, who attended college with Dr. Crump. Crawford was an airline pilot who was a race car driver, in his free time, for several years.

Roy's interest in attending NASCAR races was as strong as ever, but by 2010 Gail much preferred the peace and quiet of home to the roar of powerful engines. However, the Moodys' son, National Guard Captain Cale Moody, and granddaughter, Madison Moody, age 10 and a natural athlete, had eagerly picked up where Gail left off.

Looking back, who could have imagined that the little boy who couldn't get to the bomber crash site, and the baby who was three-months-old when his father died in the crash, would one day have NASCAR in common along with their interest in the crash history?

Readers may also be amazed at the number of computer experts and artists in various fields who were connected to the men who died on Cold Mountain.

Roy and Gail Moody (whose son Curtis was an artist), spent the night of April 17, 2010 in the Crump residence. Gail fell asleep right away, but Roy lay awake for many long hours, just thinking and marveling at being in the home of the son of Sgt. Hoyt W. Crump.

The couple's bed was near a closet which held the Army Air Force dress uniforms belonging to the Sergeant.

It all seemed surreal, and like his experience with Sgt. Merritt's albums, it touched Roy's soul in a way that time could not erase.

The time spent with Jerry and Kay Merritt and Dr. Hoyt Crump and wife Lee will be cherished forever by the Moodys.

Their only regret is that time and circumstance didn't allow them to meet Fred L. Trickey III and Dick (Okerbloom) Oakley.

Like some others in this follow-up story, Roy dealt with a number of health problems after the book was first printed in 2005.

On June 12, 2008, he visited his son, Captain Cale Moody, who was stationed in Raleigh following a tour of duty in Iraq. And the two met the author for breakfast at a Cracker Barrel restaurant between

Raleigh and the Cannon home in nearby Clayton.

The first hint of trouble came when Roy asked if the table looked odd to his companions. It did not, but to him it seemed to have become lower than when he first sat down.

He was accustomed to black "floaters" in his eyes, that looked like little spider webs, but now there was a long black "string" with what looked like an ant at the end of it. And it went up and down like a yo-yo.

Soon, he noticed something like a tiny window shade begin to lower over his eye.

Back at home, he felt he should see his ophthalmologist, but since he had a regular appointment in only two weeks, he decided to wait until then.

But the shade went lower and lower and he knew he should not wait. He learned that he had a detached retina, so surgery was performed and the vision in his left eye returned about two weeks later.

Roy had had his first knee replacement on Dec. 16, 2004, and everything went well. His second knee replacement was on January 3, 2007, and it was a different story. There were complications in the healing process, and it was eight months before he could walk normally.

As he got about with aid of a walker and a cane, he wondered if he would ever see Cold Mountain up close and personal again.

The boy within the man wondered why The Mountain had been made so unattainable, especially now that he had developed such deep connections with those whose final moments were spent there.

Then finally, on August 30, 2007, Roy Moody's knee joint "broke free" and straightened properly during one of his many bike rides.

It was on his 70th birthday.

He hiked to the bomber crash site in the spring of 2008, and returned again in spring of 2009.

Plans to make the hike with friends in the fall of 2010 had to be postponed, but The Mountain welcomed him once more in April of 2011, along with his brother-in-law, Dan Shook, and friend Bruce Taylor.

How long can he continue to visit the place where the World War II heroes died? He'll do it as long as the Good Lord allows.

As was written in the Book of Ecclesiastes: "To every thing there is a season...." and when Roy's Cold Mountain seasons have ended, springtime for another hiker may be only beginning, a hiker of a new generation who will also feel a special bond with the heroes who were claimed by The Mountain in 1946.

Roy's long-term goal in 2011, the 65th anniversary of the B-25 crash, was to fulfill the wish of a friend. He hoped to ascend Cold Mountain with his 2004 hiking companion, Gay Calhoun, on Gay's 90th birthday.

*****